Penny Taylor
Gill McKnight

Penny on Parade

Based on a True Story

Disclaimer
This is a biographical work and while the locations are correct, the names of people have been altered for confidentiality. In order to maintain anonymity, in some instances, identifying characteristics and details, such as physical properties, occupations, and places of residence, have been altered.

Cover design by Jove Belle
Photo: 32011214 © Elswarro—Dreamstime.com
Illustration: 90901878 © Mogilevchik—Dreamstime.com

ISBN: 978-1-947253-40-7

Dedication

For my mother, Dora Taylor Gartland, who believed everything I told her no matter how untrue or outrageous the stories, but above all, never reprimanded me when she found out the truth.

Acknowledgments

Thank you so much to all the women who have supported me in this journey. Alison Brown, Jennifer Jones, Andromaxi Alioptia, Tamsin Morris, Belinda Middleditch, and, last but not least, Gill McKnight.

Introduction

There's a story behind this story. There usually is.

Many years ago, I was brutally attacked and left with psychological, as well as physical, scars. Therapy became the mainstay of my recovery process, and part of that was revisiting the past and the person I had been.

It was a tough exercise and what came through was a recognition that the period of my life spent in the British Army was the making of me. I arrived a shoddy specimen and left a little shinier—but it was a hard journey.

My army memories became part of a therapy journal and eventually this book; though it tells of only the beginning, when I was a raw recruit. Raw in so many other ways, too. I'm not a hero in these pages. I'm young and scared and fumbling around the edges of my life, but I can see the me of today starting to flicker through. Even now, it's a love-hate battle.

These pages present the first six weeks of army training in Guildford Training Camp in the early 1970s.

Penny Taylor is a pseudonym.

Chapter 1

Nobody knew of my intentions on that cold, gusty morning when I walked into the army recruiting office in March 1971—least of all myself. This was my last resort. To me, there didn't seem to be a future worth having in Darlington anymore. I'd left the house early for my appointment, and now I was unsure if I'd go through with it. My heart thumped heavily in my chest as I pushed open the door.

The main office was blissfully warm and quiet. The walls were papered with posters of men and women doing wonderful and exciting things around the world in the name of Her Majesty. I gave them a brief, hopeful scan before turning my attention to the only other person in the room.

A small, wiry woman in an army uniform peered at me over huge diamante glasses that masked most of her face. I stared back, a little unnerved—the glasses were so at odds with the severity of the uniform. Her hair, too, was a curious thing—crimped to her skull down to the ears, where it suddenly took flight in a mass of bleached blond curls. Then, I realised it was a bad case of cap-hair. Out of uniform, this woman must have looked quite ordinary. In uniform, she looked like a caricature of modern army life. I was anxious enough to take this as a bad omen and considered for the umpteenth time backing out when she thrust her hand at me and bellowed.

"Good morning, Miss Taylor. I'm recruiting officer Staff Sergeant Simms."

My hair stirred in the breeze of her enunciation. How did such a small body hold so much wind?

"Mornin'," I replied quietly.

"Follow me."

We went to another office near the rear of the building. The corridor, long and painted a heavy clotted cream, had a horrid green-coloured carpet, reminiscent of pond scum, that matched Sergeant Simms's uniform. The sickly combination made me wonder about the military strategy behind pairing two wholly unsuited colours. Perhaps they were trying to drive new recruits away rather than draw them in.

She seated me across from her at a cheap, Formica wood-effect desk and opened a thick file. Her pen matched her sparkly glasses.

"Now, Miss Taylor, tell me why you want to join the army."

"My father was in the army, and I want to follow in his footsteps."

My answer was *sort* of honest. Truth adjacent, if you will. I'd follow any footsteps that led me out of this dead-end town and into a life of my own choosing. Her Majesty and her Armed Forces were my Pied Piper. I'd filled in the initial application papers the week before, so why was she asking this now?

She shuffled through her papers. "Ah, I see he was a captain." She ticked a box on the page.

Shit. Wrong father, but... "Yes."

"And your grandfather was a colonel?" She was beginning to sound excited. The army likes old blood. Another flash of the pen and another tick.

"Yes."

"So, we'll put you down for a commission."

"Um. No."

She glared over the top of her glasses, mid-tick. "No?"

"I want to join as a private."

"With your family history, you should really be considering a commission."

"I don't see my natural father or his family anymore." I shook my head vehemently. This was important to me. He'd been a brutish bully of a man. A man who resented his own children and blamed them for life's shortcomings. I'd never felt love from him as a child and the thought of claiming his legacy rang false in my mind.

Across the table, Staff Sergeant Simms's lips pursed, as if she'd regurgitated a half-digested lemon.

I persevered. "My stepdad is a coal merchant and before that, he was a private in the Marines. I want to follow in *his* footsteps."

Her attitude changed in a snap. "Well, you haven't really got enough 'O' levels for a commission, anyway."

"That solves it, then." I smiled, trying to make lemonade out of that lodged lemon of Sergeant Simms.

The rest of the interview went smoothly, and I signed up there and then.

Simms escorted me back to the front office and the street exit.

"You'll receive a letter with your start date, but as of today, you are officially in the army. Here's your service number, Private Taylor."

"Private Taylor." I sampled the words. "Sounds good." The door clicked sharply behind me and I was back out on the bustling high street.

I buttoned up my jacket against the cold.

I thought of my biological father on my way home on the bus. The last time I'd seen him was Easter 1968, when I'd visited him and his new wife. She'd resented any intrusion from his old life and made it a miserable visit. He'd bent over backwards to pacify her. *"Do you really think I'd have her here if I didn't feel obliged to?"*

My ears burned every time I remembered their overheard conversation. I left the next day with no explanation. I did things that way, I realised. Shut up, locked down, and ran away. Now I'd done it again—but to a different father. This time, I was running away from my stepdad, Ted Taylor. My mam wasn't going to be much impressed, either. I slid farther down the bus seat and watched the drab Darlington streets go by, trepidation growing.

Mam was ironing in the kitchen when I got home.

"Fancy a cuppa?" I filled the kettle and put it on the gas ring.

"Oh, yes. Please, love." She expertly folded Ted's working shirt and pulled another from the heap piled on the sofa. "Was town busy?"

"Not many about, but then it's freezing out there." I pottered about arranging the cups and sugar bowl, and brought the milk bottle out of the fridge. She was smart, my mam, and something about me put her on alert.

"Buy anything nice, sweetheart?" she asked. I should

have picked up on her tone but I was dithering, wondering how to break the news.

"I wasn't at the shops."

"Oh?"

"I went to the recruiting office," I blurted.

"Oh?" There was a hardening in her voice, as if a rebuke was quickly forming, so I rushed ahead.

"I joined the army."

The iron hit the ironing board with a thud. She opened her mouth and...nothing came out. Her eyes widened with horror and my stomach shrank. Every doubt I'd had since signing that dotted line, and why I'd done so, came flooding back to swamp me in cold, acrid water.

"You what?" she finally managed to say, as if praying she'd misheard.

"I joined up." I tried to make light of it. Bright and breezy, that was me. I looked at the paper slip Staff Sgt Simms had given me and sounded off my name, rank, and service number, perhaps a little too gleefully.

"Oh, dear God, Penny!" There was a shocked silence for a moment, then a smell of singed cotton broke the spell. "Your father's Sunday shirt!" she cried, and rushed to rescue it.

I swallowed a smirk. *Sunday shirt*. It wasn't as if Ted was a regular worshipper. He and God nodded in passing at weddings and funerals. She fussed with the shirt while I poured out our tea.

"Here." I brought a cup over, and it was only then I realised she had tears in her eyes. "Mam?"

"Penny, you're just past eighteen." She sniffed and tried to disguise her upset. "You're too young to make decisions like that. Is this to get back at him?" My mam always got straight to the point—well, her point.

I'd won a place at Loughborough University on the Physical Education course. I'd wanted to become a P.E. teacher. Mam had liked the idea. Ted, not so much. I hadn't been too young to make my own decisions then, had I? Mam had supported me, but, unfortunately, Ted refused to pay the fees in the end. Hence, the army. I had to do something.

We sat at the kitchen table, a chrome and lemon-coloured Formica affair that was my mum's current pride and joy.

"I'm out of school and need to be doing something," I said, trying to sound reasonable and grown up. "It was his choice about university. The army's my choice now." I shrugged nonchalantly, but mam had hit the target. Without financial support, I couldn't afford to go to uni.

Instead, Ted had found me a job as a receptionist at an engineering company. I'd been there for several weeks and hated it so much, I'd upped and left the prior week. The pivotal point being Jackie's funeral. I'd been refused the day off to attend—and that was that. I'd walked out. My sandwiches were still there, festering in the bottom desk drawer. Maybe they'd notice I was gone when the smell got too much? I almost giggled, then reality came crashing in. Mam and Ted didn't yet know I'd walked out. It was another fight we needed to have about my life and my future. I hated desk work with a passion. I hated a lot of things those days.

"He only did it 'cause he wanted you to stay close to home." Mam defended Ted again. It was tiresome, considering how pleased she'd been when I'd won the university place. Sometimes she spun like a weathervane to keep the peace in our house.

"I told you. It's not for me. I don't want to work in a crappy job until I get married and have a brood."

Her face closed over. I'd hurt her. It was a tiny victory and I felt a little ashamed, but it didn't make me pull my punches. Those had been Mam's only choices back then. Work or family. She'd given up work to have four children in under four years—as she was often prone to telling us kids when she was particularly maudlin for her girlhood dreams.

"Ted wants you home with us, that's all." There was little else she could say.

"Well, it backfired. I won't be at home, will I?" I was truculent now. I couldn't punish him, so I'd punish her. I'd wanted her to support me, to support my dreams. It was unfair, but I was hurting and lashed out, even though I knew in my heart that if mam had the money, she'd have let me go to university. The problem was, she couldn't understand *why* I wanted to get away. And I was in no position to tell her.

"He'll see it for what it is and be mad," she warned.

I didn't care. I was Her Majesty's property now and the Queen outgunned Ted Taylor. I wanted to leave home. To be my own person. I also wanted a decent career, and if he wouldn't help me with that, then I'd damn well find my own way. And I had. It was called the British Army. Ted may have thought he knew a woman's place, but this was the '70s and I had my own ideas.

Mam rose and rinsed the cups. I thought that was that, the first hurdle over, when her arm snaked around my shoulders and she was suddenly beside me pulling me in close to her hip. My mam wasn't a demonstrative person. This awkward bumping of bodies was her version of a cuddle. It caught me off guard and I almost started to cry. I was so raw those days.

"Will you tell him?" I asked. My courage suddenly left me, and a problem shared felt as good as this awkward, one-armed hug. Up to then, I'd been bolstered by false bravado and suppressed panic.

She withdrew her arm. "You made your own bed," she said. "I'm having nothing to do with this."

Ted came home every night at 6 p.m. on the dot for his tea. He parked his lorry at the coal yard and drove his Mercedes the half mile to his local place. There, he sank two pints of lager and placed his bets for the next day's races. He liked his beer, the gee-gees, and money, as long as he was the one spending it. He was a creature of habit.

Dinner on a Friday night was always steak and chips at the proper table in the front room, not the Formica affair in the kitchen. Mam was a creature of habit, too.

We sat around the big oak table, everyone watching the evening news on the TV in the corner. No one spoke. No one ever spoke when the news was on, except to tut at some disaster. Tonight, things were shit in Northern Ireland again.

"Well, tell him." Mam had sat quietly all through teatime. Now that the news play-out music had started, it was as if she couldn't contain herself any longer. There was a storm coming, and she wanted it to break and be over with before her TV soap operas began.

I started, surprised that she was initiating the inevitable face-off. Why couldn't she leave well enough alone? Why force a fight? I'd bring it up with Ted in my own time.

"Tell me what?" Ted asked. When there was no immediate answer, he stopped eating, his fork poised midway between plate and mouth with his last pale chip impaled on it.

My mam and I swapped glances. Ted's fork hit the plate. He straightened in his chair as his face clouded over. A forecast for the outburst to come.

"Tell me what?" he repeated in a tone not to be ignored.

"I joined up," I said. It was now or never.

"Joined up what?" He was genuinely confused.

"The dots." I couldn't resist the weak joke. Nerves, I guess.

Beside me, my mam sighed. "She's joined the army, Ted," she said, tired of my flippancy.

"You what?" He fully focused on me.

I felt like sinking lower in my seat but held my ground.

An ugly flush washed over his face right down to his shirt collar. "You fucking what?" His voice rose.

Mam began gathering the tea things. I wasn't sure if it was an excuse to get offside, or if she was worried her crockery would end up against the wall.

"I joined the army." My voice started to rise, too. "It's my life. I can do what I want."

"Not at your age, you can't. I won't allow it!"

"Well, tough luck, 'cause I already signed up." I got to my feet now, ready for a stand-up argument.

I got one. Ted towered over me. He was a big man to begin with, and years of carting hundredweight coal bags had only made him brawnier and meaner.

"As long as you live under my roof, you'll do as you're told." This was an old refrain, and I was sick of hearing it.

"I won't be under your roof for much longer."

"You won't be under my roof for one more minute. Get out!"

That's when I realised how serious it all was. Serious enough for mam to skulk in the kitchen and for Ted to throw me out.

"I'm bloody well going. Why do you think I signed up in the first place? To get away from you!"

We roared at each other across the table. It was all too much. I hadn't expected them to be happy, but considering I have an ex-military father, no matter which one you looked at, I hadn't expected this, to be thrown out of my home. To hell with them all!

I pounded on every step of the stairs up to my bedroom, dragged a nylon holdall from the top of the wardrobe, and flung every stitch of clothing I owned into it. Fuelled with angry vigour, it took less than a minute.

Raised voices lifted up the stairs to me. Mam was getting it in the neck now. Apparently, she was useless and let me get away with blue murder and that's why I was a stupid bitch just like her. Mam slammed dishes about in the kitchen, no doubt biting her tongue but furious with the both of us. All she'd wanted was a quiet night in to watch her soaps and, once again, Ted and I had gone at it, guns blazing. I felt sorry for my mam. She was always caught in between.

I thundered back down the stairs and found her waiting for me in the hallway.

"Where are you going?" Her eyes were moist and anxious, but no tears spilled over. She, at least, had accepted that I was on my way.

"To our Pete's." Brusquely, I pushed past her to the front door and slammed it behind me with the greatest pleasure.

Pete, my brother, lived in Newton Aycliffe, about fifteen minutes away by bus. Pete and I had always got on well, and I could count on him in a crisis. This felt like as good a crisis as any I'd had growing up.

I caught the Aycliffe bus and sat huddling in my misery, my face pressed against the rain-streaked glass. I accepted that there was no way things could've been different. I needed to get out of Darlington, but I couldn't explain why to my family. After Jackie, the Loughborough University course had seemed like the perfect solution. Fuck it, it *was* the perfect solution, but Ted had screwed that up royally. My life was a mess, and I had to get away. The army wasn't perfect like Loughborough, but it was a solution.

The bus dropped me and my melancholy mood at the foot of Pete's street.

"What kept you?" he asked casually, and left me standing on the doormat with my mouth hanging open.

"You know?" I came in off the street and closed the door behind me, dropping my bag in the hall.

"Mam called."

Of course she did. I was daft for not guessing. Mam would call to make sure I'd arrived safe and sound. Pete settled back on the sofa, arms crossed, half-watching football on the TV, half-watching me slump in the armchair beside him.

"So?" he said. "Tell me about it."

"I'm sure she already filled you in."

"She's upset, Penny. She doesn't understand why you did it like that. Without talking to any of them. It's a bit of a shock. She thought you were buying shoes, fer fuck's sake."

I stared glumly as Spurs got its arse kicked. Pete had gallons of patience, and so he sat and waited, his eyes fixed on the telly.

"I wanted to get away," I said, finally.

"You wanted to travel to exotic locations, meet interesting people, and kill them," he quoted the old joke. He liked playing the hippy, except he wasn't. Despite the girly permed hair, Pete was as straight-laced as they came. He worked for a car parts company and was married to Mary, who was out at bingo. Otherwise, I'd have gotten a whole lot more sympathy, and maybe a cup of tea. I liked Mary. She was kind and pretty and good for Pete. She was also strong enough to keep him out of Ted's clutches. Ted wanted Pete to follow him into business, but Mary wanted better things for Pete, like not destroying his back by humping tons of coal all day.

Buster, their bull terrier and surrogate child, lay snoring before the fireplace, happily farting every once in a while.

"Don't have to go that far to kill *some* people," I muttered, imagining running over Ted in an armoured car. Reverse, then forward. Reverse, forward.

"Is this because of your mate?" The question came out of the blue and caught me off guard.

"Who? Jackie?" I bristled. I still found it hard to talk about her and struggled to look cool, even though her name lacerated me inside. Everything cut these days, especially kindness.

He did that thing again, where he said nothing and waited.

"I couldn't get the day off to go to her funeral," I finally said. "It was last Tuesday."

"I'm sorry, Penny." There was genuine compassion in his voice. "That's rotten."

"I went anyway. I got up and walked out. Hated that effing job."

He nodded but stayed silent. I'd been too new to my receptionist job to be given time off for a non-family funeral. That had been the catalyst, I now realised. Pete had a way of doing that to me, making me think about things differently when I didn't realize that's what I was actually doing. It was at Jackie's funeral that I'd decided I had to get away.

"Life's too short," I said. It sounded trite, but it was true. Jackie would agree—and she was always trite. Always lippy and smart-arsed, a rebel going nowhere far too fast. Especially on her motorbike. Unfortunately, on her motorbike.

Pete heaved himself off to the kitchen and came back with a tin of lager. He popped the tag and handed it to me. Mary would have given me tea, but Pete—Pete got me.

"You can stay as long as you like," he said.

"It'll only be until my papers come," I said, thankful to him. I took a long swig. The cold beer felt good, and the muscles along my back and shoulders began to unknot.

"Can you change your mind?"

I shook my head. "Don't want to," I said, and took another swig.

Chapter 2

"There's a letter here for you." It was the first I'd heard from me mam, though I knew she and Pete talked regularly. They always had. They were close like that.

I stayed at Pete's for the next few days. He asked if that was what I really wanted for the short time I had left with my family. According to Pete, Mam wanted me to go back, but I refused to get off my high horse. I was sorry Mam had got caught in the crossfire but I had a right to do what I wanted with my life...and I wasn't going home again until Ted accepted that.

I fiddled with the coiled phone line, as it always twisted back into the same snarl. "Is it from them?" I asked, part excited, part nervous.

"Well, it's big and white and says 'On Her Majesty's Service' on the corner," she said. "Will I open it?"

"Don't you dare." She literally held my future in her hands. I wasn't sure what to do next. "Will I pop 'round and get it?"

"Of course, love." Her voice warmed up as if the sun had come out. I'd said the right thing. "He regrets it all." And suddenly the storm clouds split wide open and everything was bathed in warm light.

Family arguments always went like this, stormy weather followed by fair weather—except this time, I was still in a self-righteous mood.

Mam carried on. "You know how he can't ever back down. Never could. You know what he's like." Then, she added, "We miss you."

"Well, you better get used to missing me." As usual, I was too quick and said the first smart-aleck thing that came into my head. There was a damp sniff and I realised she was quietly crying. I felt immediately guilty. Did I really need an apology? This was my mam, and I'd only ever needed her to acknowledge that I wasn't entirely in the wrong and that Ted had been a prat, too. It took a lot to make Mam cry. Okay, so I was the baby of the family, but surely it shouldn't be that hard for her to let go? I was itching to move out and start a life of my own, and as far as I was concerned, that was the normal thing to do. All my friends were leaving home—why couldn't Mam and Ted see that, too?

"We love you, pet. Come on home," she said.

"He threw me out, so he needs to ask me back. And

we both know that's not going to happen." It could have been so different. They should have been proud to have a kid at university. Instead, they had tried to shut me down and look what happened—I found the army. I had needed Ted to fund my college place, a mistake I wasn't going to repeat. My new career choice offered me independence and I was grabbing it.

"Can't you come home and talk it through with him?"

"No. My mind's made up, there's nothing to talk about. My answer is in your hand in a big white envelope."

"I should burn it," she said vehemently.

I broke out in a sweat. "Don't do that! He's an ex-Marine. He'll go ballistic if you damage Her Majesty's stationery." It was a guess, maybe even a lie. For all I knew, Ted didn't give a stuff about the military anymore, but I wanted that envelope, and Ted's possible reaction gave her pause for thought.

"So, when are you coming over, then?" She changed tack. "I can do a nice dinner. What do you fancy?"

I felt the walls of their neat little semi closing in around me.

"Better yet, Mam, just redirect it."

"**A**pril fifth."

"That's quick." Mary lifted the chip basket out of the pan of hot oil.

"Not quick enough." I placed a knife and fork for each of us on the table, along with the salt and pepper.

"Do they know?"

"Mam does. I've no idea about him."

"What's the point of being so stubborn?" Mary shook the last of the fat drips from the chip basket before tipping the lot out onto our plates. We were having fish fingers, chips, and peas.

"You're as bad as he is," Pete chimed in. He lifted the plates over to the kitchen table, where I had just finished setting out the condiments. Pete, Mary, and I were rubbing along well, except Pete always wanted everyone to be happy and sort things out, while I preferred to sulk and fester.

"She always takes his side." It was an old whine, and one that had served me well over the years.

"She's the one living with him. You managed to get offside and leave her with the flack." Pete always took Mam's side. I tried not to let it annoy me.

"He's the one who needs to apologise to me."

We sat down at the table and I reached for the ketchup. Pete snorted and tucked into his dinner.

Later, after Mary and I washed up and we all settled in to watch television, someone knocked on the front door. Pete went to answer it, and Ted followed him back in. He looked upset, and I immediately turned down the volume on the telly.

"What's happened?" My hands began to tingle. "Is Mam all right?"

"It's yer Aunt Lily," he said. I immediately felt relieved. I knew what was coming next. Aunt Lily, his sister, had been terminally ill for some time.

"She passed on this afternoon." Ted confirmed what I'd guessed.

"Oh, Da," I said and gave him a hug.

He was genuinely grieving and clung on tightly.

"Will Christine cancel the wedding?" Pete asked. Christine, my cousin, was due to be married in a few weeks. Lily had been Christine's mother.

I stepped out of the hug, wondering at the answer.

"Christine says she'll go ahead. It's what her mother would have wanted." He turned to me. "Your mam and your Auntie Vera are going down to Chichester for the funeral. I can't leave work. They've asked if you'll go along, too?"

Of course I would. Aunt Lily was a favourite of mine and I wanted to pay my respects.

The next day, I moved back home and helped my

mam organize the growing number of family who wanted to travel with us to Lily's funeral.

The rift had been mended and no one had apologised. It had always been that way. A fight came, a fight went, and nothing was never addressed. Just eclipsed by a new, more pertinent drama.

Christine and Alan's wedding fell on April 4, and the family descended on Chichester again, only this time en masse. I could understand why people preferred a wedding to a funeral; still, it was sort of cheeky to make it to one but not the other, considering they were so close together.

The bride looked beautiful in her wedding gown, and it was particularly poignant, as Lily had bought it for her. Unfortunately, Alan was Catholic, and Christine had agreed to marry in his church. It was an extra-long service compared to what us Methodists were used to. On our side of the aisle, family members grew twitchy. Everyone was gasping for a cigarette, and once the bride and groom had paraded down the aisle to Mendelsohn's "Wedding March," the Taylors nearly trampled the flower girls to a pulp in their rush for a fag break.

Pete and I, and Alan's younger brother, Kenny, sneaked

around the side of the church behind some ornamental bushes for a puff, making sure we wouldn't inadvertently pop a cloud of smoke into the background of the wedding pics. A few minutes later, Ted joined us. Things had begun to thaw between us over Lily, and when he offered me a cig from his own packet, I knew we'd be okay. Ted did things glacially slow. It was like making up with an iceberg.

The wedding photo session took forever, since there was so much family on both the bride's and groom's sides. But it was fun to be outside of the oppressive church and know the best bit of the day still lay ahead. A big, boozy reception.

This was held in Shipham's Social Club. Christine worked at Shipham's and so we had use of the upstairs room, plus a free jukebox. In no time at all, the beer was pouring and I was on the floor grooving with Kenny and my grandad to Neil Diamond's "Sweet Caroline." I felt a pang for a moment. It had been Jackie's favourite song. I missed her and wondered how my life would be now if she'd not died. Would I still be twenty-four hours away from a new life in the army, or could we have maybe worked something else out?

I went outside with Kenny for a cigarette. I'd decided to stop once I finished this packet. If I was serious about a career as an Army Physical Instructor, I'd need my lungs.

"Why'd you want to go join the army?" he asked.

I shrugged. "Nought else to do. I hated my job and can't afford college. I'm hoping the army will pay for my education." I sounded smarter than I felt.

"So, what you want to do?"

"Be a physical instructor."

There was an awkward silence, and I realised he didn't know what that was. Kenny was sweet and about the same age as me. He'd just landed an apprenticeship as a brickie, and his family seemed pleased for him. He wasn't that bright, and bricks would be good company for him. To reinforce this impression, Kenny chose that moment to lean in unannounced and give me a big, slobbery, beer kiss that thankfully slid off my mouth before it could attach itself. I imagined this was what an Alpine rescue by a St. Bernard must be like, only with beer instead of brandy.

"Penny." My mother came out to join us. I'd never been so glad to see her since popping from her womb. Kenny scarpered with a guilt-stricken look on his face. At least he had the sense to get offside quick. Mam gave me a weird look, and I knew she'd witnessed the kiss. But she said nothing, bless her.

"It's a good night, isn't it?" I said as she drew alongside. "Lily would have loved it."

"That she would," my mother said. It wasn't cold, so

I was surprised when she wrapped her arm through mine and drew in tight.

"Are you coming to see me off at the station tomorrow?" I was travelling from Chichester to Guildford, and the Women's Royal Army Corps—WRAC—training camp the following morning.

"Course I will."

"Will Ted?"

She shrugged. "He'll be hung over."

So would I, but I planned to sleep mine off on the train.

"Penny," Mother continued in a cautious, caring voice that made me pay attention, since I'd heard it so little before. "You will be careful, won't you?"

I wasn't sure what she meant. "It's okay, Mam. They don't let us play with guns in the WRAC. The men do the fighting. We're the back-up forces. It's not as if I'm going to shoot my bloody foot off."

She tutted, "I don't mean guns. I mean...leslibeins." She stammered over the word and sounded embarrassed. *Leslie Beans? Who's that? What the hell is she on about?*

"Oh." I suddenly got it. "It's *lesbians*, Mam." I burst into nervous laughter. She withdrew her arm and sniffed. She didn't find any of it funny.

"I'm just saying. The army's full of them."

"You'd think that'd be where you'd go to find a man,"

I said jauntily, though inside I felt a bit squiffy.

"Is that what you're about?" she said, a little too sharp.

I decided this conversation, like all our conversations, had only one way to go: downhill. It was best to change the subject now. Or, better yet, stop talking to each other altogether.

"Come on, lady." I grabbed her arm again. "It's cold out here." It wasn't, at least not to me. "Let's go inside and have a dance, eh?"

Mam came with me to the station the following morning. Neither Pete nor Ted made it out of bed, since their heads were too bad. I was glad about that in the end. It was nice that it was just Mam and me, although we didn't talk during the journey to the station. She didn't mention "leslibeins" again either, and I was glad for that, too. She bought me a Ribena, a ham sandwich (because "British Rail food is daylight robbery"), and a *Jackie* magazine. I'd rather have had one of the new *Cosmopolitan* magazines, since they suited my age better, but my mam thought they were filth.

I initiated a farewell hug, grabbing her by surprise moments before leaping on the train. I waved goodbye as it pulled out of Chichester Station, and can still remember the lost look on Mam's face, as if maybe she was missing me already.

Chapter 3

Guildford train station was far larger than any I'd ever been through before. People came and went in floods. Intimidated, I stood for a moment, suitcase at my feet, and wondered where the hell all these people were going. And why did they have to get there so fast and with such rudeness? I was bumped and jostled several times and nearly fell over my own luggage.

I noticed an exit with less of a crush and went that way. It led out to a quiet street. Unsure what to do, I used my suitcase as a stool and waited for "them" to come and get me, as per the instructions in my letter.

The longer I stayed there, the more uncertain I felt. I gazed anxiously left, then right, then left again, on the lookout for the bus that was to take me to Guildford training camp. Was I the only one arriving today? There was nobody else waiting—only a constant stream of coming and going, and none of it army-looking.

Half an hour later, when my anxiety had reached crisis point, another girl appeared. She walked up the street, lugging a big brown suitcase that was almost as big as her. She looked as lost as I felt.

She shyly approached and settled on her own suitcase a respectable yard or two down from me. I stared, expecting her to at least introduce herself. After all, we were both perched on our cases like broody hens, obviously waiting for something to happen. But she said nothing and simply stared back with owlish intensity. Her dark brown eyes had too much white around them, giving her the intense, slightly mad look I was now subject to. She had mousey hair with wisps easily escaping her hairpins, and her coat hung half-on, half-off her shoulders, with one blouse collar sticking up. In short, she was a great, ruffled brown blob, what Pete would describe as "disarrayed" and I would call a whacking great mess. She could have as easily fallen out of a hayrick as gotten off the train.

"Who are you waiting for?" I asked. One of us had to go first and it might as well be me. She didn't reply so I continued, happy to chat because I was nervous. I always gabbled on those occasions. "I'm supposed to be joining the army today, and I've been waiting for the bus for half an hour now. I don't know where they've got to."

Her eyes lit up with relief. "I'm joining the army, too." Her broad Geordie accent was welcoming. "I'm Mandy."

"I'm Penny. Are you from the North East?" Sort of obvious with that accent, but I wanted to keep the conversation going.

"Yeah. Are you?" Clearly, she'd picked up on my accent, too.

"Yeah. Where are you from?"

"South Shields. And you?"

"Bishop Auckland. Me nan comes from South Shields, though. It's a nice place," I said.

Seems Mandy agreed it was a lovely place and far too good to leave, because she burst into tears.

Oh, my God. I hope they're not all like this. I fumbled for a tissue and kept talking, trying to change the subject. How could someone be homesick when they'd only got as far as the train station?

"Like I said, I've been waiting over half an hour. I think I'll go see if I can phone the camp and find out what's happened to the bus." I stood to go. "Will you look after my case?" I asked, a little uncertainly.

Mandy's face was buried in my tissue and she seemed a bit unfocused. I didn't want to come back to a missing suitcase and no Mandy. A wet burp and small nod made me feel confident enough to go exploring. I ducked back into the station to find a public phone box, fumbled about in my bag for the army letter, and dialled the number under the address.

"Guildford camp guardroom," a bored voice answered.

"Hi, I'm at Guildford Station waiting for the camp bus and it hasn't come yet. What should I do?" I was nervous and the words all ran together. I sounded giddy and garbled.

There came a sigh. "What street exit did you go out of?" The jaded response told me this was a frequent query.

"There's two?" I squeaked, inwardly cursing my lack of control over my voice.

"Yes."

"Sounds like I used the wrong one."

"Fancy finding the right one?" With that, she hung up on me. At first, I was miffed at the rudeness, then I realised I hadn't given my name and cheered up. I may have been stupid, but I was also anonymous.

I hurried back to Mandy and grabbed my suitcase. "We're at the wrong entrance. Follow me."

She stood obediently.

"And don't you *dare* tell anyone we were waiting at the wrong gate, got it?" I ordered. She nodded rapidly in agreement.

We retraced our steps back through the station to the platform. From there we found the proper exit and the elusive army bus, which couldn't be missed for those who used the correct way out. It was already filled with other girls, and rows of pale faces lined the windows. We picked up our pace and a uniformed woman appeared at the door glaring at us impatiently. Even at this distance, I could make out the insignia of a corporal. Knowing army ranks was going to be a great advantage, I realized. This happy little blip was short-lived. The scowl on the corporal's face deepened with each step we took. My stomach dropped. Clearly, we were the last two and everyone was waiting for us. I felt sick with nerves.

The corporal pointed to the rear of the bus and said with a tight snap, "Luggage over there!"

Mandy and I rushed to comply. Cases stowed away safely in the boot, we went back to the bus door.

The corporal was whipcord thin with a long, pointed face and sharp nose. Her hair was pulled back into a severe bun that did nothing to soften her looks. She reminded me of Judy from the Punch and Judy puppet show. It was an unfortunate coincidence, for now she had entered my mind as "Judy."

"Name!" she bellowed about two inches from our faces.

Beside me, Mandy looked as terrified as I felt. "Mandy," she whispered.

"Mandy *what*?" Judy bellowed again. She could have

frightened a bull. "You're in the army now, girl. You and I are not, and never will be, on first-name terms. You left 'Mandy' at home, understand?"

"Y-yes."

"Let's try again, shall we? Name!"

"T-Turner."

"That's T-Turner, *Corporal*." She mocked the stammer. "Do you see these stripes on my arm?" She pointed to them. "That means you call me Corporal, get it, Turner?"

"Yes, Corporal." Mandy slithered onto the bus with a scarlet face and burning ears. I was glad she had gone first. Judy turned to me next.

"Taylor, Corporal," I said before she could yell at me.

"Move yourself, Taylor. You've kept us all waiting." She thumbed toward the bus steps. I was up them in a shot, following Mandy to a free seat near the rear, passing the sea of sympathetic faces on either side. Everyone looked slightly shaken. I assumed they'd all gone through something similar.

"That's the way to do it," I quietly mimicked the squeaky Judy puppet voice as I slumped into my seat, buoyed by a surge of relief. The joke was practically nonexistent, but it served to defuse my anxiety somehow.

Mandy let loose a raucous peal of laughter. Alarmingly loud.

"It's not that funny." I tried to hush her.

Judy stood glaring from the front of the bus, trying to identify the mirth maker. Mandy and I simultaneously slid farther down our seats and tried to look straight-faced and innocent. I don't think we fooled Judy, but nothing else was said on the journey to the training camp.

Guildford sped past the bus windows, as unremarkable as any large English town, until we turned onto the street that led to Guildford training camp. Houses, shops, and trees were rapidly replaced by wire fencing with barbed extensions at the top.

"Christ, it's a prison," I muttered.

Mandy sat wide-eyed and fell silent. She'd been bending my ear all the way over, exclaiming about this and remarking on that. Once she'd gotten over her nerves, she'd become an incessant chatterbox who'd managed to bring on the beginnings of a tension headache for me. I'd wanted to sit in peace and absorb it all, not listen to inane, nonstop twittering.

The bus paused at the main gate in front of a red-and-white barrier. A female guard in uniform with a black RP armband for the Regimental Police came out of a sentry box and lifted the gate so we could drive on through.

"I wonder who she's in mourning for?" Mandy mused.

I gave her a sharp sideways look to see if she was joking. She wasn't. She'd really misread RP as RIP. Mandy was as green as a field of frogs, and not for the first time, I gave thanks that I came from an ex-army family and had a little knowledge for these things.

"She's in mourning for us." I grinned, playing on Mandy's innocent remark, then went on to explain. "RP means Regimental Police."

Mandy snorted, but with subdued laughter this time. Neither of us wanted Judy's attention again.

Guildford training camp was massive. A little town all to itself. As we drove through the camp, you couldn't miss a large tarmacadam parade square that I knew we'd soon be getting very familiar with. A two-storey office building sat opposite the parade square and a large building I guessed to be the cookhouse. The bus headed uphill toward several three-storey buildings, obviously our accommodation blocks.

No sooner had we swung in and the driver pulled on the handbrake, Judy was on her feet yelling. "Hurry and get that luggage unloaded. This bus needs to get back to the station to collect the next lot." On seeing our blank faces, she sneered. "Did you darlings imagine you were the only ones?"

Once the bus had made a smart turn and departed, Judy split us into four groups, divided alphabetically by surname. "...Stewart, Sutcliffe, Taylor, Teague, Turke, Turner..."

Mandy and I ended up in First Company, Platoon 3, or 1Coy, 3Plat.

One Coy Platoons 1 and 2 were led away by another non-commissioned officer, or NCO, to one of the dorm blocks. NCOs came up through the ranks, whereas commissioned officers joined up with a set of stripes. That's what I'd turned my back on with Staff Sgt Simms at the recruiting office.

Judy stayed with us. "Right, you lot, listen up. This is Block B. I'm going to allocate your rooms. Three Plat are on the top floor. Tea is at 1700 hours in the cookhouse. That's the big brick building we drove past down the hill," she yelled, though we were only a few feet away. "At 1800 hours, we meet in 3Plat office. That's here, on the middle floor. Got that?" Didn't anybody speak at normal volume in the armed forces? All the yelling felt so unnecessary.

A few feet away, 4Plat was getting an ear-bashing from its own corporal. They were located in the same building as us, only on the ground floor.

"Yes, Corporal," we said meekly in unison. I could understand how the constant shouting wore down all resistance.

"Follow me." Judy proceeded to dispatch us, floor by floor and room by room. Each room held four trainees. Apart from the narrow beds, we each had a bedside locker, along with a small wardrobe. This was to be home for the next six weeks. She unceremoniously dumped 4Plat on their floor, and the rest of us headed for the stairs.

"Middle section is Platoon Admin," Judy thundered as we dragged our luggage up the stairwells. "To the right, NCO offices, to the left are platoon offices."

By the time we reached the dorm rooms on the top floor, most of us were out of breath and the contempt for our lacking fitness was visible in Judy's eyes.

"Up here," she said, "your dorm rooms are to the left and NCO rooms are on the right."

The NCO quarters were conveniently behind a set of swing doors and tucked away out of sight. She began allocating rooms. We were told to stand in the hallway until called forward. Mandy and I were the only ones left as each room was allocated a full complement of recruits. Finally, Judy pushed open the last door, number two, and thumbed us in.

"Taylor, Turner, in here." She moved off, completely disinterested, now that her chore was done.

"Yeah! We were meant to be together!" Mandy dumped

her suitcase, grabbed me into a massive bear hug, and did a little hop-and-skip dance.

"Ahem." Two other girls watched in amusement from their beds. I wriggled loose, face flaming.

"She's excitable." I flung my suitcase on the nearest empty bed. "I'm Penny, and Prancer here is Mandy."

"Carol." A tall, fair-haired girl, who spoke with a lovely Irish lilt, rose and shook our hands. She was in her early to mid-twenties—older than any of the other recruits I'd arrived with. "And this here is Joan." She introduced the other girl in the room.

"Hi," Joan said. She was thickset, with a strong handshake and a Brumie accent. "So, you two know each other, then?"

"We only just met at the train station," I said.

"But it feels like years ago," Mandy added chirpily. Yes, it certainly did.

"We came in earlier this morning," Carol said. "If you want to unpack now, maybe we can all go over to the cookhouse together."

It seemed like a good idea. Not that there was much to unpack. My suitcase was small, and I was ready to go in about fifteen minutes. We all waited while Mandy fussed over her toiletries. She had an inordinate amount of soaps and bubble baths, all still in gift boxes.

"My family bought me pressies," she explained. The boxes took up more space in her case than her actual clothes.

"Why didn't you leave the packaging behind?" I asked.

Mandy squeezed an empty cardboard box to her chest. "It's part of the sentiment," she said. I was beginning to suspect Mandy was one cog short of a full working mechanism.

After shooing Mandy along, we ambled over to the cookhouse shortly after five o'clock and joined a long queue of girls in civvies waiting to be fed. The cookhouse was partitioned, us on one side and the NCOs on the other. When I finally reached the food hatches, I was disappointed by the choice. The selection was meagre, the portions small, and the food as good as inedible.

"I'll be thin as a stick if this is what they're feeding us for the next six weeks," Joan grumbled.

I pushed my plate away half empty and went to stock up on chocolate from the vending machine in the corner. I agreed with Joan, except I was already stick thin. I had a wiry, strong build that needed constant refuelling. If I didn't eat regularly, I got headaches and felt sick. Back home, they'd just be sitting down to one of Mam's dinners. What would it be? Beef stew and dumplings, or sausages and mash? For the first time, I felt homesick.

Dissatisfied and hungry, we headed back to our block for the meeting at six o'clock, or rather, 1800 hours. I had to start making all these little mind-set adjustments. Our platoon office just about managed to hold all thirty-two of the new recruits in 3Plat. We huddled nervously, speaking in low voices, eager to see who our platoon leader would be and what the training schedule looked like.

The door snapped open and a small, neat woman entered. We fell silent at once. She was a lance corporal, and she took one of the seats behind the desk, leaving the main seat free. That meant someone else was due. The lance corporal studiously ignored us, adding to the air of unease.

The door opened again, this time with a flourish, and Judy breezed in. I groaned inwardly. Were we going to be stuck with her?

"Quiet!" she bellowed.

We all shut up.

"Right. I pulled the short straw and got you rabble," she began, dumping a load of pamphlets on the desk. "In case you need to be told all over again, I'm Corporal Hacker and this is Lance Corporal Adams. We are in charge of 3Plat—that's you lot." She passed out the pamphlets. "This tells you all you need to know about the camp, your training, and what the army expects from you. Learn it well!" There was a rustle as we passed the papers around the room. Judy continued. "Do what's expected and you've got a future here. Mess around, and I'll have the skin off your backs, understand?"

Silence.

"UNDERSTAND?" she roared.

"Yes, Corporal." We were finally getting the hang of this.

She waved a pamphlet. "Anyone wanting to ring home and boo-hoo to mummy can check the map on the back. The phone boxes are marked in red. Do it now. Bed check is normally at 2200 hours, but tonight I want you all tucked up by 2100 hours. Lance Corporal Adams and I will personally come around to wish you all sweet dreams."

There came a loud rustling as everyone turned over their pamphlets and eagerly scoured the map. Judy paused, then continued. "You will now follow Lance Corporal Adams while she issues your bedding. She will then show you how we expect your bed to be made. Tomorrow you go for uniform fitting. I want to see you gathered outside Block B at 0830 hours. No trousers. Only skirts or dresses to be worn. Got that?"

"Yes, Corporal."

Everyone filed after Adams to a storeroom and gathered a bedding bale. Then, we followed her to the nearest room, where she patiently instructed the owner of the bed on how to make it, while we all crowded in and watched. It was a bit of an anti-climax for my first army lesson. I already knew how to make a bed. This one had sharper corners and neater tucks, but basically it was the same routine. We were sent off to do the same thing with our own bedding.

Once I'd made mine, I spread out on it and quickly read the pamphlet. If there was a common area where we could go mingle and relax, we weren't aware of it yet. I knew there had to be somewhere set aside for downtime. A NAAFI bar or tearoom. It was a relief when I found one and pointed it out.

"What does NAAFI mean?" asked Mandy

"Navy, Army, Air Force Institution. They run the shops, bars, and cafes for us, I told her. "If we want breakfast before 0630, we have to inform the cookhouse the day before," I read aloud. "I'd rather eat this pamphlet."

"We're not allowed off the camp for two weeks," Joan moaned. "So, no nipping out to the chippie. I'll starve to death."

"The map is pretty handy," said Carol. "At least we know where everything is."

"Does it show you the escape routes?" Mandy giggled, and we all forced a laugh. It was a pretty depressing read. It took us about twenty minutes to get through it all.

"So, who wants to phone home?" I asked.

"My mam's not on the phone, so I think I'll stay here and write her a letter." Joan gave a heavy, homesick sigh.

"My lot haven't a phone either, so it's a letter for me, too," Carol said.

Mandy and I left them to it and headed off to the NAAFI that had a red mark next to it on the map, indicating a phone kiosk. The queue for it went out the door and onto the street.

"We'll never reach the phone by nine o'clock," I said, pointing out the obvious. "Let's have a drink instead." I'd noticed the NAAFI bar off to the left.

"Okay." Mandy headed toward the cafe.

"Not a cup of coffee. A real drink." I pointed in the opposite direction.

"Okay," Mandy chirped, and did a neat 180-degree swing for the bar door. As she turned, she bumped into Donna Sutcliffe, who was heading for the cafe. Donna was also in 3Plat and had the room next to us.

"Where are you two going?" she asked.

"For a pint in the bar," Mandy said. I could have kicked her. There was something about Donna I didn't like at a gut level. She reminded me of a girl I'd been to school with, a right snitch.

"I don't think Corporal Hacker would approve of

that," Donna was quick to point out, making my guts do the cha-cha.

"Don't care. She'll never find out anyway," Mandy sing-songed, blithely unaware she was making an enemy. Mandy had no nose for trouble, whereas I could sniff it a mile out, and Donna had me gagging. I tugged Mandy's sleeve and we moved off.

"I don't trust that one," I muttered. "She's a tattletale."

"Oh, Donna's all right," Mandy answered, confirming my worst fears.

The smoke-filled NAAFI bar was dingy, with dark wood furniture combined with a sticky, heavily patterned carpet, and faux leather upholstery that had seen better days. There were a few people, but not many for this time of night. I took little notice of them anyway, making a beeline for the bar. Everyone appeared to be in couples having a drink.

"What do you fancy?" I asked Mandy.

"Arrived today?" the barmaid called over.

"Yes," we replied in unison, though our civvie clothes and green grass attitude said it all.

"I'm sorry, but I've got to ask. Are you both eighteen?" She came closer to give us the once-over.

"Well, I am," I said. I looked at Mandy. "Are you?"

"Yes." She sounded offended.

The barmaid was satisfied. "Okay, then. What do you want?"

"Two pints of lager, please."

"They don't like you being in here." The barmaid casually poured our draughts.

"Who doesn't?" Mandy asked.

"Your training NCOs don't."

"We're not allowed?" Mandy asked, alarmed.

"Oh, there's no rule. They just don't like it, is all."

"Well, tough!" I grabbed my pint and took a long drag of my cigarette. I resented being made to feel chaperoned and scolded. It was as if I hadn't left home at all. After I paid and turned away from the bar to find a free table, I realised Mandy and I were the centre of attention. It was intense, unwelcoming, and strangely embarrassing.

"They should be in the milk bar." I heard a snigger from a nearby table but ignored it. Our information pamphlet said that we were not allowed to talk to permanent staff. "Permies" were soldiers of all ranks who staffed the camp, from trainers to administrators, medics, drivers, catering, anything you could think of to keep Guildford running like a small, self-contained village. Some permanent staff were soldiers who had completed training and were in H&D division—Holding and Drafting—waiting for their deployment papers.

Guildford acted like a holding tank for soldiers between transfers. The sniggerers at the next table were obviously permanent staff, so I held my tongue.

We found a table at the back, sank into the lumpy, vinyl upholstery, and relaxed. It wasn't until we'd been there nearly half an hour that I realised that everyone in the bar was female. And they were all in couples. I was agog and couldn't take my eyes off them. Jackie and I had always met in bars. We were discreet and careful, and I sensed an undercurrent in this one that made my pulse quicken.

Mandy was oblivious, chattering away about the ups and downs of the day while I cast sly sideways glances all around me, feeling like a stranger in a world where I knew I belonged.

Chapter 4

The clang of a bell woke me. I sat up in a blind panic—was there a fire? Judy threw open the door and stood on the threshold, viciously shaking a hand bell. For a split second, I expected her to scream for us to evacuate the building because of "Fire!" or "Flood!" or "Locusts!"

Instead, she yelled, "Get up! Get dressed! Get breakfast! Now!" She disappeared down the corridor to bellow into the next room and give those occupants a heart attack.

"Is she mad?" Mandy asked.

"That's the way to do it," I mimicked the Judy puppet's squeaky voice. It cheered Mandy up immensely. She was an easy audience.

Our room was small, but the four of us perfectly choreographed moving around, making our beds and getting dressed. The next orchestrated part was to get to the ablutions, or washrooms and toilets, at the far end of our floor, before the mad morning rush started.

Breakfast at the canteen was as miserable as the previous night's tea. They offered cold toast, over-brewed tea, and cereal with powdered milk on top. Across the partition, the NCOs had proper milk sitting on their tables, and I made a mental note to buy my own as soon as possible.

At 0830, we gathered outside Block B and milled around anxiously. Down the hill, on the main road, we could see Platoons 1, 2, and 4 being organised into some sort of order and knew something big must be happening. Sure enough, Cpl Hacker arrived followed by LCpl Adams. They quickly formed us into three lines ordered by height with the shorter girls sandwiched in the middle. This was an old marching trick to make the platoon look taller all around. Since I was tall, I was made to lurk near the back.

Coming up the path towards the dorm blocks, we could see four uniformed women, all with three sergeant stripes on their sleeves. They walked purposefully toward each block, splitting off as each reached her allocated platoon. The shortest sergeant plodded on to us. She was a diminutive, bespectacled woman who reminded me a little of Recruiting Officer Simms. I wondered if she'd be any quieter. No such luck. Her opening words nearly blew us off our feet.

"I am Sergeant Manners. And *I* am the only person in your sad little lives you need to worry about. Keep me happy or I will squash you!" She looked at us like we were something stuck on the sole of her highly polished shoe. "My job is to mould you into soldiers fit to serve in Her Majesty's Armed Forces. And from where I'm standing, I don't fancy your chances. Do you get my drift? You are sloppy. You are undisciplined. You are the most miserable bunch of useless dross that ever crawled into this camp." She looked over to Judy and shook her head solemnly, as if they were well and truly lumbered. Then, she swung on her heel and stormed off down the hill.

Quite frankly, we were shaken. How could we be failures so soon? We'd only arrived less than twenty-four hours ago! We needed more time to be a miserable bunch of useless dross.

"Turn to face me!" Judy barked. We swivelled in a disorderly mass. Judy sighed. "First things first," she said. "You need basic drill training to stop you looking like idiots around here. Lance Corporal Adams will demonstrate the essential commands."

"'Ten'shun!" LCpl Adams bellowed, and a few minutes later we knew how to come to attention and stand at ease. The other three platoons were doing the same and the walls of the accommodation blocks echoed with shouted drill commands. We then added left and right turns to the mix. This continued for another twenty minutes until we were deemed reasonably decent enough to be seen out marching.

"We are now going to march to Q store for your uniforms," Adams told us. "I will start you off with the command, "By the left. Quick march. On the word 'march,' put your left foot forward and march. You stop on my order: 'Halt.'"

All four platoons set off more or less at the same time but it soon became obvious we all had different destinations. One Plat went off toward the education block, 2Plat headed for the gym, while 4Plat, poor buggers, went directly to the parade ground to continue this torture for the next couple of hours.

Processional caterpillars have probably made it down to Q store quicker and with more aplomb than we did. After several stops and starts, we finally made it.

Q store was on the lower floor of the large office building. It stored every damned thing a WRAC would ever need from enormous, armpit hugging knickers to safety pins and shoeshine. Item after item was heaped upon us until I thought my arms would break. In predictable army fashion, we received actual kit bags to ram everything into near the end of the process, and not at the beginning when it would have been more useful. The army, I realised, was a huge beast not geared to easily facilitate the common soldier, or sometimes even common sense. It pleased itself, and I had to figure out how to march along with it and not get squashed.

I recognised some of the women who had been drinking at the NAAFI bar the night before, but everyone was too busy to make eye contact or share a friendly gesture, even had I been brave enough to make one.

We were also measured for our uniforms in Q store. Somewhere behind me in the queue, Mandy brought the entire hall to silence with a panicked cry of, "Don't touch me!"

I looked back over my shoulder. One of the butch girls from the NAAFI bar had approached her with a measuring tape and now blinked at her stupidly until an officer came over to see what the hell was going on. I was mortified and hurriedly moved on to the next hatch to collect two pairs of the ugliest shoes in the world. As soon as we were kitted out, we had to walk back to our block weighed down with our new kitbags. Mandy was waiting for me outside.

"Did you see that queer trying to touch me up?" she said.

"No." I hadn't time for Mandy's histrionics. This time, she wasn't even mildly amusing.

"She did, Penny, honestly."

"How do you know she's gay?" I refused to use the word "queer."

"We saw her in the bar last night, dressed up like a man in trousers and everything. Remember?" Mandy was eager to find a fellow condemner, but I hung back.

"Who?" I pretended indifference.

"She was with that lot sitting opposite us. At the NAAFI bar?" Ah. So, Mandy was more observant than she let on.

"Look, Mandy, I think you're mistaken, she was only doing her job, not coming on to you." I picked up my pace and left Mandy behind. She never mentioned the Q store girl again.

After lunch, dressed in our new uniforms, we gathered in our platoon office for a talk by Sgt Manners. LCpl Adams was there to greet us.

"Find somewhere on the floor and sit down," she ordered. We didn't have to wait too long before Manners and Judy entered and took their seats at the desk.

"Now then," Manners practically cooed, which should have been a warning. "Let's have a friendly little chat."

Her eyes were like flint. "Now, I'm not a demanding woman. You'll find worse than me here. But I do have some expectations of you."

I felt as if a boa constrictor had hold of me and was slowly tightening its coils. Manners had a way of making the room feel airless.

"During training, the platoons compete for three cups," she continued, surveying the room to make sure she had one hundred percent attention. "There's the Drill Cup. I have won this cup a *few* times," she gave a little shrug, "and it would be nice if I could win it again. The same goes for the Physical Education Cup. It's a nice little trophy, but looking at some of you, I don't think I've got much chance there." There was some awkward shuffling as the criticism sank in. Manners paused to let it sink deeper before carrying on. "The Accommodation Cup, on the other hand, is the most prestigious of all—and it's mine!" There was a stony silence after this.

After a prescribed time, she continued. Manners knew theatre. Her timing was impeccable. "It has *always* been mine and it always *will* be. I don't care how I win it or what you have to do to win it for me, but win it I will!" Her voice was getting louder and harder and adding to our unease. Then her tone changed. It became weary, dejected, quiet. She was freaking me out with all these mood swings. It was psychological warfare wrapped up in friendly fire.

"Unfortunately, at this moment in time, I can't see that happening." She gave a sad little headshake and a theatrical sigh. Then her head snapped up and she pinned us to the floor with an acidic glare. "And why is that, you ask?"

We hadn't. At that moment, none of us dared to even exhale loudly. We sat still, breathing through our noses, as constrained as constipated mice.

"Well, I'll tell you why. Because winning the Accommodation Cup requires *discipline* and *respect* and you lot haven't got either!" She suddenly bellowed, making us start. "This is your second day here, and you still haven't grasped the fact that when a senior rank walks into the room you stand, get that? You stand even if you're on the bloody toilet!" We looked at each other in amazement.

"'Ten'shun!" she roared. There was a lurching scuffle as we all tried to stand up at once, but we were so crammed in we knocked each other over in our rush. People went arse over tit throughout the room. Judy grinning from ear to ear at the debacle. It was a planned procedure to rattle and humiliate us, and I hated them for it. What was wrong with a little "please and thank you"?

"That's better," Manners said calmly once we'd all attained an upright position. "Next time do it immediately." And with that, she walked out, leaving us in a state of bewilderment.

Judy stood before us, an evil glint in her eye. "Now you're going to learn how to iron," she said. "The army has kindly provided you with a lovely, brand new uniform, and you're damn well going to look after it."

We began a shuffle toward the door when she called, "Taylor, Turner. Remain behind."

My stomach dropped. Mandy looked at me as if I had the answers. I glared at her, hoping she had the sense to keep her mouth shut during whatever came next.

"A little birdie told me you two slid off to the NAAFI bar last night," Judy began reasonably. "There is to be no fraternising with the permanent camp staff. Is that understood?"

I knew it. Donna is a brown-nosed snitch. Sneaky bitch.

"Be aware I know *everything* that goes on in this camp," Judy continued. "I can smell trouble from a mile off, and I smell it off you two." She thrust her face within an inch of ours. She was so close I could smell the salt and vinegar crisps on her breath, which, believe me, smelled worse than trouble.

"I'm keeping my eye on you, be warned. Now get out

and join the others." She dismissed us with a curt nod of her head. We spilled out into the corridor.

"Wow. She really does know everything," Mandy whispered in hushed reverence.

I looked at her, amazed. Mandy might be a good laugh, but she was also as thick as cookhouse porridge. I decided not to mention that Donna was a cow. If Mandy couldn't connect the dots, I'd leave her to her ignorance. I'd already tried to tell Mandy how it was with Donna, but she'd refused to hear it. There was no point repeating myself now. She had to work these things out for herself. But now I had Donna's number, and I'd be careful around her in the future. I also knew we were allowed to use the NAAFI bar just as we used the cafe or the shop. Judy's private interpretation of the rules was intended to disqualify alcohol while on training, and *that* would not work for me.

They separated us into two groups for the ironing demonstration and, fortunately, Adams was in command of the group I was in. Surprisingly, some of the girls didn't know how to iron. Adams demonstrated on her own kit, showing us how to press a uniform and iron a shirt. All the while Donna shot me sly glances from across the room. No doubt she was itching to know what Judy had said to us. Let her wonder for a while. Mandy was sure to pour her guts out later, but my business was my own.

After the demonstration, we were given the rest of the afternoon off to iron our own kit properly. As there were only three ironing boards between thirty-two of us, I suggested to Mandy that we should take a well-de-served coffee break. Several other girls thought this was a good idea, so we headed off to the NAAFI cafe. Mandy had heard of a Christian coffee bar on camp called Re-deemers, and wanted to try that out, but we couldn't find it. I didn't tell Mandy, but I was secretly relieved.

"Did you hear anything last night?" Mo asked. Mo was the nickname for Maureen Tanner, a popular girl who bunked across the corridor in room one.

"No. Why?" I asked.

"We thought we heard the ghost," Mo answered.

"*You* thought you heard the ghost," her roommate, Doreen, said and laughed. "Then she woke the rest of us up in a panic. I couldn't get back to sleep again because she had us in such a state."

"What ghost?" Mandy was google-eyed.

"Yeah. What ghost?" This was news to me.

"Block B is haunted," Mo said. "A girl hanged herself on the top floor years ago. And she wanders along the corridors at night."

"She does what?" Mandy looked horrified.

"She rattles the door handles and tries to get in your room," Doreen said eerily.

"Who told you this garbage?" I asked.

"A girl in 2Coy," Mo said. "It's a true story. A recruit did kill herself on our floor."

"Would they let us change floors, Penny?" Mandy asked me. "People who commit suicide are sent to purgatory. Maybe that means you're stuck as a ghost where you...you know...killed yourself?"

"There's no such thing as ghosts. I'm staying where I am. You can go ask Judy to change your room, and good luck to you." Ghosts didn't scare me, but the thought of a suicide on our floor did give me the willies. In the misery of the moment, that felt very possible.

Chapter 5

The first week passed in a flurry of square bashing and domestic duties. We had been taught how to iron our uniforms and "bull" our ugly shoes. There was an art to bulling leather shoes, which took an enormous amount of work with a damp cloth and shoe polish. In the end, you had to be able to see your face in the leather. Meanwhile, the standard of cleaning expected in the accommodation block was impossible to achieve, especially as the block was in constant use. We were being exploited as cheap cleaning labour, and I was exhausted.

A few days into week two, and we were marched in three file to MRS, the Medical Reception Station, for our inoculation injections. This was not a popular outing. All the platoons were there, and we formed an orderly queue, shirt sleeves rolled up. Doctor Fraser, the camp Medical Officer, gave us our jabs while several nurses did the paperwork.

I found myself giving my name and number to a very attractive blonde. I blushed vividly and felt stupid under her steady blue-eyed gaze, so much so that I fluffed my army number and felt Judy scowling at the back of my head. We were supposed to know our rank and number by heart before we even arrived at camp, and here I was, stumbling over it because of a pair of pretty eyes. The nurse dropped her gaze to her documents but not quick enough to hide the small smile that popped a dimple in her cheek. She was gorgeous. I gave a weak smile, which she totally ignored, and moved along the queue toward the doctor.

As we marched up the hill on a hot day with stiff, sore arms, we were in no mood for LCpl Adams's haphazard commands. She'd made a few errors on the way down, much to our amusement, mainly getting her left and rights mixed up. Now it was tiresome and annoying. It was hard enough learning the drill without having a duff instructor.

We approached a T-junction, knowing full well we had to swing left. Sure enough, Adams muddled it and had us turning right into a hedge.

"Halt." Red-faced, she regrouped us, and we took off again, but not before a few sideways looks had been swapped between me, Doreen, and Bridget, the leading soldiers of each file. Being among the tallest, we were regularly placed to the fore for marching drill. By uncanny agreement at the next swing, where Adams duffed it up once again, the right file led by Doreen swung right, the left headed by Bridget went to the left, while I and my central file marched on in a straight line. We reckoned at least one file would be going in the correct direction. I thought it hilarious, a real kickback at all the crap I'd been put through these first weeks. But half a dozen steps in, it was Carol who yelled, "Halt!"

Adams stood white-faced behind us, stunned. Her eyes teared up, and she swiftly turned away from us.

"Get back in file," Carol ordered through gritted teeth. She was fuming with us and suddenly I felt very small and mean. Of all the NCOs in Guildford, Adams was easily the nicest, and we'd just made a public fool of her. We quickly shuffled back into order and stood to attention awaiting the next command.

"By the left. Quick march." It came in Adams's voice, and we moved off, marching the best we'd ever done.

Back in our block, Carol gave us all a bollocking. "Do you think we looked clever? Would you have done a stupid prank like that on Judy? It was cowardly and we're better than that. I saw Adams getting painkillers from the nurses. She suffers from migraines and that's why she gets her commands fluffed time to time. Her head is killing her. You all need to back off, understand?"

We understood. We really did. From then on, Adams got the utmost respect and that extra mile from our platoon. Carol, much to her consternation, became our adopted spokeswoman. Being older and more mature than the rest of us, we looked to her for direction. She wasn't particularly comfortable with it, but she was always there for anyone who had a problem.

The thing I looked forward to the most was a visit to the NAAFI bar whenever I could rustle up someone to come along with me.

Mandy wasn't so keen now that she suspected the bar was full of queers ready to ravish her at any moment, though I could usually cajole her along. She was pliable like that. However, the next time Mandy and I returned, I could tell she'd been recognised as "that crazy bitch from the Q store incident," and I was embarrassed to be seen with her.

Most of the others were leery of breaking the no-fraternizing-with-the-permie-staff rule. I pointed out that we didn't fraternize—we never spoke to anyone other than the barmaid, and she was a civilian. The truth was, my friends were too frightened of Judy to risk it. I couldn't blame them. I was nervous of her wrath myself, but the excitement of hanging around "those" women always got the better of me.

One evening, Carol joined us, more for a look-see than anything. It was a relief to have another body there. Before, if I'd wanted to use the loo, Mandy had insisted on coming along. She was too uncomfortable to sit alone at our table. Or, if she needed to go, she'd whine for me to accompany her, in case someone accosted her in the toilets. It was tiresome and felt like kindergarten. Plus, I didn't want anyone to think we were a couple. Not that I was there looking for anything...or anyone. I was simply there to look, to feel somehow involved—though only on the periphery.

With Carol in tow, I could at least nip off to the loo on a solo mission and leave her and Mandy yakking. One evening I walked in on a conversation that two girls were having by the hand basins.

"...has taken the lead. She's six points clear." Laughter, then, "Dirty bitch. Who's your money on now?"

I recognised one girl as the pretty nurse from the MRS inoculations day. The other was a stranger to me. I tried to catch the pretty nurse's eye, so we could maybe share a smile. I suppose I wanted some reassurance that she liked me, too. She flicked me a cool glance in the mirror. I felt crushed and a little bit silly. She and her friend shut up the minute I appeared and stayed silent even after I entered the farthest cubicle to offer them privacy. I could hear the rasp of the hand towel dispenser and then the swish of the door as they left. They had clearly been talking about a bet. Gambling was forbidden on campground and I wondered what they'd bet on.

Back at my table, Mandy and Carol were ready to leave, so I finished the last of my beer in one gulp and headed back with them.

The next morning started with another platoon meeting with Sgt Manners.

"Next Thursday is 2Coy's Passing Out Parade. You will be in attendance and hopefully realise what all this hard work is about."

There was a buzz of excitement. We would be witnessing our first POP, Passing Out Parade. Once 2Coy was gone, we would be the senior recruits and a busload of sprogs would roll in behind us. It would be nice not to be bottom of the heap.

"I want you all to turn out as smart—no, *smarter*—than they are. Therefore, on Wednesday morning there'll be a kit inspection, and heaven help you if your kit isn't up to scratch." Manners paused to allow the information to sink in and the fear to grow.

Satisfied with the level of discomfort, she continued slowly, but as usual, gaining in volume. "Tonight is your first 'In night,' and that is exactly what it means. You will stay in and clean the block until it sparkles. Tomorrow morning, Lieutenant Perryman and I will inspect your work." Lt Perryman was the commissioned bigwig in our little world. "I can promise we will go over each room with a fine-tooth comb." Manners descended into a growl before finishing in a crescendo. "So buck up!" Some of us actually flinched.

"Corporal Hacker will allocate block duties to each of you," she continued in a normal voice. "That will be all. Dismissed." Turning on her heel, she stalked out and we let loose a sigh of relief.

It was short-lived as Judy stepped up to the mark. She had a clipboard and read out various duties on the rota, and assigned each duty to a room number.

"Room two." She came to our room number and looked up. "You lot are on the ablutions. I want you to clean them thoroughly." She turned to leave, then hesitated and added an extra word of advice. "Make sure to go over them again in the morning. You wouldn't believe how dirty things can get overnight."

"Yes, Corporal," Mandy, Joan, Carol, and I sang in unison.

"Ablutions has to be the worst job of the whole bloody lot," I complained the moment we were on our own. "She hates us. It's a waste of time doing them tonight. We might as well wait until early morning."

"We can't do that, Penny," Joan said.

"Why not?"

"Judy will be watching us. If she says do them twice, she means twice."

"I can't stand that woman!" I exploded. Judy was worse than a hundred Ted Taylors. She had more power over me, too.

"Well, there's nothing we can do about it for the next five weeks, so hang in there," Joan pointed out.

I thought about the problem while I bulled my shoes. "I suppose we could clean the majority of the cubicles tonight, then close them off. Then we can finish the rest in the morning?" I suggested. "What do you think?"

"Bloody good idea, Penny," Carol said. "But we'll have to check with the rest of the floor and see if they mind."

"We can only ask," I replied.

"It's worth a try." Mandy leapt to her feet. "I'm going to ask."

"If they give you any problems, just remind them they'll have to clean them in turn. So, what goes around comes around," I told her.

Mandy wasn't away long. "They told me to piss off."

I was surprised. "Who did?"

"I went next door to Donna's room and they told me to piss off."

"Well, what did you expect from Donna? She's so far up Judy's backside, she's practically a haemorrhoid," I said.

"Come on, let's all go." Joan was on her feet. "No one talks to room two like that."

"Yeah. Let's call a meeting and get everybody together," Carol said.

"Where? There's thirty-two of us," I said.

"In ablutions," suggested Joan. "It's the biggest room, anyway. Come on, let's round everybody up."

The first room I went into was Mo's, across the hall. "Hey, everyone. What have you got to work on tonight? We've got the ablutions." I pulled a face and got some sympathetic looks back.

"The ironing room," Mo answered.

"You jammy bastards. You won't have to clean that again tomorrow. You could close the door and ban everyone from using it."

"We can't do that. Someone might have ironing to do."

"At this time of night? Hardly likely. We'll all be slogging away on our chores," I said. "Meanwhile, we'll have to clean the ablutions twice, since we can't stop people piddling. It's fucking ridiculous."

"Our turn will come," Mo said, and walked into my clever trap.

"How about we help each other by creating a few new rules?" I asked ingenuously.

"What's your game, Taylor?" Mo's eyes narrowed. Such lack of trust wounded.

"Room two proposes that we clean half the ablutions tonight and close that section off. Then we'll clean the other half in the morning." I paused, waiting for a response. I got none, so I continued. "We can't do this unless we all agree." Still no response. "How do you feel about that?"

"Seems a good idea to me," Mo said and checked with Brenda and Elaine, her roommates, who shrugged their okays. "Doreen's gone to the loo but she'll agree, too. We should all help each other on these In-nights."

"I'm scared stiff of Manners, and we don't know what she'll do if the rooms aren't up to scratch," added Elaine.

"I know," I said. "We really should organise something that would make In-nights easier. Joan suggested that we all meet up in ablutions and see how everybody else feels. Are you in?"

"Okay," Mo said. "Let's get everyone to meet in fifteen minutes."

By the time I'd rounded everyone else up, the ablutions were full. I was one of the last to arrive and the room went quiet with expectation. Everyone turned to face me, and I realised they were waiting for me to say something. I hadn't reckoned on being the spokesperson, but seeing how everyone needed me to be one, I suddenly felt swell. I was up for it. I took the plunge and leapt onto a bench.

"Okay, everyone," I began. "At some point in the next few weeks, we'll all rotate our In-night duties." I let that sink in. "So, basically, each one of you in turn will have ablutions to do. Tonight, it's room two's turn, and we know you'll all want to shower after you finish your jobs, and go to the loo throughout the night, and that will undo all our cleaning efforts. Okay?"

This brought a rumble of "so what?" and "not our problem, mate," as expected.

"Quiet!" I roared, taking a leaf from Judy's book. It worked. We were all so conditioned that everyone immediately shut up. The control felt exhilarating. I found a new confidence inside myself. "What I suggest is that we clean and close half the ablutions at 2000 hours. These will remain out of bounds, okay? Then, in the morning, we'll clean the other half after everyone has finished their morning wash." I waited for a response but there was a wall of silence, so I continued. "I also want the entire ablutions locked down after 0730. That will give us the time we need to finish them off."

The grumbling began again until I found an unexpected ally. Mo came to the front and shouted, "Room one is shutting off the ironing room at 2030 hours, so anyone got ironing to do, better get on with it now." There was no room for argument in her voice, either. We were laying down the law for Block B.

"Anyone else?" I asked from on high. I needed to nail this down before I left my perch. It was agreed with room three that corridors and stairwells would be deep-cleaned that evening and afterward, everyone would wander around in sock soles until the morning. Room four, Donna the snitch and her crew, had the laundry, or washroom, as the army called it.

"I suppose, if everybody had their kit prepared beforehand on a Sunday, then there'd be no need to use the ironing room or the washroom at all on In-nights?" Donna said, thinking aloud. That cracked it. If anyone was going to thrust a stick in a spoke it would be Donna. She was a natural-born objector. Now it looked as if she was on board, and that meant the meek and mild would follow. Until Donna landed her whammy. "But what about the NCOs? They use both facilities. Who's gonna make them follow the new rules?" She looked directly at me in challenge.

I accepted her challenge and leapt nimbly off the bench. "All we can do is ask."

As expected, Donna baulked at actually going down to the NCO offices, but good old Carol went with me. I was glad for her level-headed support. The NCOs tended to give Carol more deference since she was that bit older than the rest of us.

"You'd better leave the majority of the talking to me, Penny. You haven't really got off to a good start with Corporal Hacker."

"I'm not going to argue with that."

We found Judy in the NCOs office.

"Corporal Hacker, could we have a word with you, please?" Carol asked politely. Intrigued, Judy pushed open the door to the office. LCpl Adams sat behind her desk doing paperwork. She looked up, equally surprised, and smiled, relieved when she saw we weren't bringing trouble.

"It's like this, Corporal. We thought that if we closed off half of the facilities during In-night, then we could clean those areas thoroughly, leaving us with less to do the next morning."

Judy looked pleasantly surprised. "Congratulations, Private Turke," she said. "We don't normally come to this arrangement until the third week. I knew as soon as I saw you that you had initiative."

"Well, actually, Corporal, it wasn't my idea," Carol said and nodded towards me. Judy's smile disappeared. "It was Private Taylor who came up with it. That's why she came with me."

"Still, nice to see your initiative rubbing off on the others." Judy couldn't give me any credit. It stuck in her craw to praise me. I honestly didn't care if Carol got the glory—I only wanted an easier chore list—but it was interesting to see how personal Judy got with her grudges.

"I'll agree to your request. However, I can't speak for the other NCOs, though I don't think they'd disagree."

"Should we inform Corporal Evans?" Carol asked. Cpl Evans was in charge of 4Plat, which occupied the ground floor of Block B, though her private room was on the same floor as ours, beside Hacker's and Adams's rooms.

"Don't worry about telling her. She'll agree," Judy said. She turned her back on us. "Now get out, I'm busy."

"Thank you for agreeing with my suggestions, Corporal." I couldn't resist rubbing it in and wisely left before she broadsided me. LCpl Adams followed us out.

"Congratulations on the quick thinking. It's a sort of test. You'll make a good platoon yet, but make sure you don't let the other platoons know what you're doing."

Adams smiled. "This is a competition, after all, and you know how determined Sergeant Manners is on winning." She gave a wink and wandered off toward the vending machines. "Oh," she called over her shoulder, "maybe best to talk to Corporal Evans about this, okay?"

We got the message. *Don't take Judy's advice.* If Cpl Evans shared the same block as us, we needed her compliance, too. There was obviously a competition within a competition among the platoon NCOs. Everywhere I looked on camp, there were gambling schemes and all sorts of side bets.

"I think we need to find Corporal Evans directly," Carol said. "Adams is right. I'd rather we did everything correct and orderly. We can't afford to have another corporal pissed at us. Having Judy in a snit all the time is bad enough." She paused thoughtfully and looked at the long corridor of closed doors. "I wonder where she might be."

I burst out laughing. "Follow the singing."

Carol frowned.

"Evans is Welsh," I explained. "She's always singing." Sure enough, a lovely contralto was wavering across the hall toward us. "That's coming from 4Plat office." I took off in that direction with Carol in tow.

"How do you know it's her?"

"Haven't you noticed her on the drill square?" I said. "She sings the marching orders out to her lot. That's why they're so good at drill—she gives them a beat to learn their steps to, like dancing." I was smug at my revelation. I'd noticed this a few days before and thought Evans, for all her geniality, was a clever woman. I'd have much preferred her as our NCO than sour gob Judy.

Cpl Evans was surprised we'd sussed the In-night chores so quickly, but she agreed to our idea about cordoning off part of the top floor for the rest of the night.

Carol and I reported our little victory back to our platoon. It looked like we were seriously ahead in the race for the Accommodation Cup.

Chapter 6

I fell sick that weekend. An aching pain in my abdomen came on very suddenly on Sunday evening and had me almost on my knees. Judy wasted no time in having me dispatched to MRS to see Dr Fraser. Joan helped me hobble over to the MRS night entrance. She rang the outside bell and we hovered under the overhead door light until a nurse appeared.

I was in such discomfort, it didn't matter that it was the lovely blonde nurse I had a crush on.

"What's wrong?" She unlocked the night door and ushered us in. The clinical smell of hospital corridors hit me and made me even more bilious.

"Corporal Hacker sent her over. She's got bad stomach pain," Joan said.

"Pain in belly," I mumbled. "Feel sick." It was an effort to talk—even like a cave man.

"Come with me." The nurse shooed Joan back out and grasped my upper arm. "Tell Corporal Hacker that Doctor Fraser will be in touch." She locked the door on

Joan's startled face, then led me to an examination room. "Up on the couch."

I needed help to even do that. Before I could say thank you, a thermometer was stuck in my mouth. "Put that under your tongue." She was very no-nonsense, though to my fevered mind, she looked lovelier than ever. On reading my temperature, she went over to the desk, lifted the telephone receiver and dialled.

"Sorry to bother you so late, Doctor Fraser. Nurse Scott here. We've just had an admission." She listened for a moment, then said, "Abdominal pains. Ninety-nine point six." She listened again, looked across at me, and reported, "Greener than week-old fish. No rash." She turned back to me. "The doctor will be along in a few," she said curtly, then left me lying there while she clattered off down the corridor to fetch me a glass of water. I didn't want one, but she was determined I have it anyway.

Dr Fraser, Guildford's MO, was there within five minutes and embarked on a quick and embarrassing rectal examination, which thankfully happened without the attendance of Nurse Scott, or Nicola, as I'd found out. Dr Fraser preferred first names rather than rank. He then declared, in his marvellously vague way, that I maybe had a grumbling appendix.

"Let's keep an eye on you overnight. If the temperature's gone in the morning, we'll send you on your way."

With a jolly "cheerio," Dr Fraser left. Nicola helped me off the examination couch and back down the dimly lit corridor to a small ward of six beds. All empty.

"Is he always so bleedin' cheerful?" I asked. Nicola smiled, and I was glad I'd been brave enough to start a conversation. "He retires later this year, so, yes, he's very bleedin' cheerful." From the bedside locker, she produced a white cotton gown that laced up the back. "Here. Put this on."

Then, much to my embarrassment, she watched me undress. My fingers were extra fumbly and I managed to make a mess out of nearly every buckle and button. Nicola snorted in amusement and brushing my hands out of the way to take over. She was quick and efficient and had me down to my bra and super-sexy army knickers in no time. My face flamed. Between this and the rectal examination, it had been a humiliating night.

Whatever the look on my face, Nicola took pity and held up the gown between us, effectively shielding my tattered modesty. "Drop the rest of your clothes and climb in."

My knickers and bra landed by my bare feet and I slid my arms through the gown armholes. Of course, the final indignity was that I couldn't reach the ties around the back, so Nurse Scott had me turn around so she could truss me up. I scrambled onto the high bed like a tot on Christmas Eve, not missing the sly smile Nicola gave my bare backside as I slid between the sheets. She'd enjoyed it, I realised. This was a game to her. The realisation gave me a thrill that rippled through my newly pain-free belly and sat tingling a little lower.

Again, my face betrayed me. She laughed, making her dimple pop, and I crushed out on her even more. I was a little high, and I liked it.

"How about a cup of tea?" she asked, picking my clothes up off the floor.

"I'd love one." I settled back on my pillows, relieved to be free of stomach pain, and happy to have even a little bit of her attention.

When she returned with a cup of strong tea, she fussed around the ward, folding away my clothing into my bedside locker and chatting amicably about nothing in particular.

"Are you the only one on duty tonight?" I asked.

"Yes. Nights can be boring." She perched on the side of my bed. "I was glad when that bell rang," she said, referring to my and Joan's arrival. "And I'm glad it was you."

She gave a sideways glance that made my stomach flip.

"Though, I'm sorry you're feeling rough."

"I'm feeling better already." I smiled like a fool. It was true. The pain was easing. "Has the MO told Judy I'm staying in?" I asked anxiously.

"Judy?"

"Oh, sorry." My face flushed again. "It's our nickname for Corporal Hacker. You know, from the Punch and Judy puppet show." The moniker had caught on, and everyone in 1Coy was using it now—except Donna and her cronies, of course.

Nicola snorted. "Good one. She looks like a Judy," she said. "So, who's Punch?"

I hadn't thought of that. "We don't have one."

"Well, annoy Sergeant Manners and you'll have one, all right."

That made me immediately anxious. Manners had us wound up like springs about her damned Accommodation Cup. I broke out of my miserable reverie with Nicola's cool touch on my forehead.

"You're still feverish," she murmured.

"That's you," I mumbled, and could hardly believe my own ears. What the hell! Why had I said that? What was wrong with me?

Nicola laughed. Her hand stilled, and her thumb smoothed across my left eyebrow. *Was that a caress?* My heart hammered in my chest. She seemed to consider something, then lowered her head and kissed me full on the lips. I was in shock—for one second—then I was in delirium, a beautiful nirvana, swimming with sensation, and totally breathless.

She pulled back, leaving me bereft. "I'm sorry. I shouldn't have done that." She looked mortified. I felt mortified, too, but for a different reason.

"Don't." I muttered.

"I'm sorry," she apologised again, distressed.

"No. I mean don't…" What? What did I want? "Don't stop. I liked it."

She stared at me hard, perhaps a little surprised, then burst out in a delightfully raucous laugh. "There aren't many of you to the pound, are there?" she said. "You're a natural flirt, Private Taylor."

This was news to me. A natural flirt? Personally, I felt slack-mouthed and stupid, like a newly landed fish.

Nicola rose from the bed. "You've been noted down at the NAAFI, but I think they don't know the half of it."

She smiled roguishly and I grabbed for her. I wrapped her in my arms, pulled her in tight, and kissed her. I was rough and passionate, and she froze for a second, and in that second, I panicked. Had I misunderstood the situation? Was this the wrong thing to do? Maybe she didn't like me as much as I liked her. And then, suddenly, she was kissing me back.

I was amateurish and awkward, and unsure how to kiss. Jackie and I hadn't done much besides a few quick, clumsy kisses. I so desperately didn't want to get this wrong. I pushed my tongue into her mouth and she pulled back laughing, wiping her mouth with the back of her hand. "Down, Fido."

"I kiss like a dog?" I was devastated.

"No, you fool." She hoisted herself onto the bed and stretched out beside me. "You kiss like a horny soldier, but we can work on your finesse." Her smile was the most beautiful thing I'd ever seen. She was lying beside me, her face inches away from mine, and it felt like the sun had come out and warmed every inch of my body.

Her fingers teased into my hair, until she had fistfuls of it. Gently, she pulled me to her and whispered, "Let's do it my way this time." And we kissed again. Softly, with building intensity. Her tongue was like silk, tender and teasing. She tasted of mints that failed to mask the cigarette smoke. She was wonderful.

"I've had a fancy for you from the first time I saw you," she said.

"Me, too," I said. "Though, I wasn't sure you even noticed me."

"You learn to hide things like that here."

Her words were curious, but I didn't care to enquire further. I was too busy being lost in the blue of her eyes, her soft breath, the lovely bloom of her flushed cheeks. We lay on our sides while she casually plucked loose all the ties on the back of my hospital gown and trailed warm fingers along my spine. I moaned. This was delicious. My thighs were damp, and I squeezed my legs tight to prolong the deliciousness.

At the base of my spine, her fingernails drew lazy circles across my bottom until my flesh goose bumped with pleasure. Then her hand trailed across my fluttering belly and up to cup a breast. I just about exploded when she squeezed, and I groaned into her mouth.

"Do you like that?" she whispered and stroked my nipple.

I whimpered incoherently.

"Sorry, what did you say?" She flicked it playfully and I gasped. Then, she unexpectedly gave it a pinch.

"Ow."

"Oh? You don't like that?" Her eyebrow quirked.

Nicola liked games, and I wanted to play these games with her. On this bed. Forever. She stroked my nipple tenderly again, as if to make up for the rough treatment. "But you like this?"

"Y-yes," I hissed. I was so close to coming I was practically incoherent.

Nicola dragged the bothersome gown off my shoulders and straddled me. Her uniform rode up and I ran my hands along the firm curve of her stocking-clad thighs. She kneaded my breasts, not once breaking eye contact with me.

I arched my back and tried to make contact with my aching hips.

"Naughty." Her punishment was to squeeze both nipples until I cried out, in lust and pain. I had no longer any idea what I felt. My body was on fire and my hands were trapped by my sides, pinned by her knees. "Tell me you love it."

"I love it," I cried. My nipples were on fire. Nicola leaned over and kissed me. She reached down between her own legs to my sex. I was soaking wet and her fingers skilfully slipped between the folds and touched my clitoris. The tip of her finger had barely touched me when I came hard in a writhing mess.

I lay in shock, heart hammering, breath desperate and ragged. Aftershocks of my orgasm ricocheting around my body. I was dumbfounded. I had often masturbated to a climax, but this...sweet Jesus. I thought I'd died.

Nicola slithered off me with a satisfied smile. She lay

beside me and feathered loose strands of hair off my sweaty brow.

I reached for her hand. "I never... I didn't..." I ran out of words and breath.

Her smile dropped away, and a sincere but surprised look replaced it. "That was your first time?" she asked incredulously.

I nodded. "I knew I liked girls, but... I've only ever kissed before." Once again, words failed me. I felt a complete mess. My heart was still doing the rumba behind my sternum.

"Oh, baby, I wish I'd known," she murmured and ran a dry, cool hand over my cheek. "You act such a smartarse I thought...well, it hardly matters what I thought now. Here." She poured me some water from the carafe.

"Always the nurse, eh." I took it gratefully.

She laughed and brushed a lock of my hair back in place. "Not necessarily," she said, her blue eyes flashed wickedly, "at least, not for you." I was sold. She could do anything she wanted to me as far as I was concerned.

Nicola retied my gown and tucked me in bed like a kid. She gave me a chaste kiss on the forehead, also like a kid, and left me. My head was woozy, the pills were taking full effect. With gargantuan effort, I managed to force my eyes to stay open to watch every little move she made.

Long after she left the room, with a little air kiss for me, I lay and stared at the door, going over every detail of what had happened between us, until I fell asleep.

The rattle of the curtains being torn apart and bright daylight cutting through the window woke me most unpleasantly. I squeezed my eyes tight against the light.

"Good morning, sleepyhead." The greeting came from an unfamiliar voice.

I cracked open one eyelid and was momentarily confused. Where was I? Then, it all came rushing back in gut-churning detail. Nicola. Sex. In the cold light of day, I was uncertain what to make of it all.

The nurse bustling around my room was not the one I wanted to see.

"Where's Nicola?" I asked, "I mean, Nurse Scott."

The nurse paused for a fleeting second and gave me a curious look. "She's off duty. It's 0900, and Doctor Fraser will be here soon to see you."

"When will she be back?"

That must have sounded needy because her face soured.

"She's off for three days. She's just done a block of nights."

She never said goodbye. Contrite, I shuffled upright in my bed. "Who are you?" I changed conversational direction. I wanted to know if Nicola had left me a message but realised that would be unlikely, not to mention a dangerous thing to ask.

"Nurse Wilson," she said sharply, "but you can call me Cherie, seeing as how you're on first-name terms with Nicola and all."

I didn't like the "and all" bit. It was laced with peevishness. Cherie was small, with a thin, knowing face. She scuttled about like a rat, doing a bit of this and a bit of that and making it all look like a big deal. About the time she'd finished rearranging all the things on, and in, the bedside lockers—which had been perfectly placed beforehand—I noticed a breakfast tray abandoned on a nearby bed while its contents grew cold.

"Is that mine?" I pointed at the tepid tea and the toast with the congealing butter, and, best of all, a soggy bowl of cornflakes with *real* milk.

"You're the only one here." Her reply was meant to be saucy but only annoyed me. I'd had shit breakfasts since I'd arrived at Guildford, and now this twit was sabotaging my only chance to have a decent one.

I scowled, and she brought the tray over, dropped it on my over-bed table, and wheeled it up to me. I lost no time in devouring cold tea and toast, as well as the soggy cereal. I was starving.

"Wow, you were hungry." Her voice held a little remorse.

"They feed us crap," I said with my mouth full.

"I can bring you more tea and toast, if you like." She softened like butter.

I gave her my best smile. "That would be lovely." I was almost flirtatious. To be honest, I'd have married whoever had keys to the kitchen. I was sick of filling up my hunger pangs on chocolate from the vending machine. In fact, I suspected that's what gave me a bad stomach the night before—I'd been eating too much rubbish.

It's not like I was being unfaithful to Nicola, I thought. Flirting for food is bona fide soldier behaviour.

Five minutes later, Cherie returned with a steaming mug of tea and a plate piled high with buttered toast. Butter—not the stinky margarine we got at the cookhouse. I sort of loved her for a moment, and it must have showed, because she smiled knowingly.

"You get great food in the MRS," she said. "Same as the officers' mess. We're having pork chops for dinner tonight."

I moaned. I loved pork chops. The nearest we got to them was cheap, grisly sausages.

"With applesauce and mash," she continued, clearly enjoying the torment on my face, but in a way that didn't feel malicious.

"What's for lunch?" I asked in the vain hope I might be around for it. I'd only two and a half hours to fill… and if the doctor was late on his rounds?

"Cheese omelette with those round fried potatoes."

My heart broke in two. No Nicola and probably no omelette with round fried potatoes. This was an awful day. I could have cried.

"Do you think you'll be leaving, then?" Cherie asked, seeing my defeated face.

"Well, my stomach doesn't hurt anymore." I eyed my empty plate, the proof of a healthy digestive system in the crumbs before me. "And my fever's gone." I knew I was grousing, but really…cheese omelette.

Cherie sighed. "You're the only patient today. It's boring when there's nothing to do."

Misery likes company, so I joined her in a round of what-might-have-beens. "We could have played monopoly, or cards, or something."

"If you had a temperature, old Fraser would keep you in, especially as we're not busy."

She sighed even harder and took my tray away. Two minutes later, she was back with another mug of hot tea and set it on my bedside locker. I eyed it carefully. I'd just returned from the loo and wasn't certain I wanted more tea. It always went straight through me.

"Cherie?" A call floated down from the reception area. It was a man's voice.

"That's him. He won't stay long. He's got golf later with the gynae consultant from the civvie hospital. You can imagine the hole-in-one jokes." She rolled her eyes and made for the ward door. "Coming, Doctor Fraser," she called. "I'm just taking the patient's temperature."

She handed me the thermometer and I looked at her in confusion. Surely, she should pop it under my tongue? I went to do so myself, but she frowned and glared at the mug of hot tea beside me.

"I hope your temperature hasn't spiked any," she said, loudly enough for the doctor to hear, and left to go find him.

I had a light bulb moment and grinned. *Cheeky little mare.* I dipped the thermometer in the tea and listened for the sound of approaching footsteps. Sure enough, I could hear their chatter as Dr Fraser and Cherie headed towards my ward. At the last possible moment, I popped the thermometer out of the tea mug and into my mouth and sat there innocently, hands folded on my lap—ignoring the growing tea splash on the chest of my gown.

It was too late to do anything about it anyway. They'd entered the ward.

"And how are you this morning, Private Taylor?"

Why do doctors always address you when you have a thermometer in your gob? I smiled and wiggled the glass pipette in his direction. On cue, he seized it and squinted at the tiny numbers through his glasses. Cherie went on tiptoe to spy. "Has she eaten any breakfast, Nurse?" he asked, sharply.

The question sent her down to the flats of her feet. "Just the tea, doctor." She nodded at the mug by my shoulder. It was a blatant lie and I adored her for it. But it was dicey. Too high a reading and I'd be rumbled. Too low, and there would be no cheese omelette for me and no monopoly for Cherie today.

His eyes narrowed—for all I knew he was half-blind—then his gaze darted to the tea mug and to my chest and its tea stain. His lips thinned. My stomach sank. And then, his thin lips quirked into a big smile.

"I think we'll hang on to you for another twenty-four hours, Private Taylor. Just in case." He didn't even examine my stomach. No pressing, no probing. Thank God, for I wasn't sure where and when to fake a moan and the last thing I needed was to fake appendicitis and end up in surgery. There was no mention of painkillers, either. I suspected the old goat knew I was a sly one and didn't give a rat's rectum about it. He'd be gone on full pension in a few months, so why should he worry about a raw recruit's extra day in bed? Fraser was a top chap, as far as I was concerned.

"See her NCO is informed." He handed the thermometer to Cherie, scribbled on the clipboard attached to the foot of my bed, and was out of there in seconds flat, heading for the fairways.

Cherie gave me a smug grin. "See? Told you so." And went off the find the playing cards.

We played poker most of the morning, and I decided that working in the MRS must be one of the jammiest army jobs ever, between the sex, the food, and, from what I could see, lying around doing very bloody little. I started to wish that I had nursing experience, so I could at least have considered being a medic.

I tried to wheedle more information about Nicola from Cherie, but her face always went sly whenever I tried.

Cherie was a card shark. I'd always considered myself pretty good at poker, but she ran rings around me. Thank goodness it was only for matchsticks.

"Good job this isn't strip poker," she said once, giving me a sideways glance. "I'd have you bollock naked several times over."

I plucked at my hospital gown. "Big deal, you'd only have to win one hand. I've naught on under this."

Around noon, she went to the front desk to receive the lunch trays she'd ordered earlier. It was the best cheese omelette I'd ever tasted, and the fried potatoes were fab. No wonder so many of the officers had a spreading waistline.

I wanted to have a snooze after my lunch and tidied the cards away. After all, I had to make the most of this idle time. Cherie took on another of her sly looks. She had a million of them.

I'd settled back on the pillows, happy to daydream about Nicola and all that she'd done to me until sleep—or masturbation—claimed me, when Cherie banged into my ward, pushing a small cart with various sponges and towels and a huge bowl of steaming water.

"What the hell?" My lazy turned-on daydreams went pop.

"Bed bath," she announced, and gripped my bedclothes.

"What?" I hung on to the blankets tightly. "It's half past two. Who gets a bed bath in the middle of the afternoon?"

"You get a bed bath when the nurse says so." A tiny tug of war ensued, which I lost. Cherie may have been short, but she was wiry and ruthless. Before I could register the bedclothes piled at the foot of my bed, she'd descended on my scant gown, expertly pulling the back ties open. I clutched it to my chest like a Sabine woman.

"Stop this nonsense." There was salaciousness in Cherie's face as she ran her gaze over my barely covered body.

My nipples hardened under her bold stare.

"My shift ends in an hour and you need to be washed before Staff Nurse Doherty comes on duty. She's a stickler."

Something in me changed gear. Her eyes glinted with a promise I wanted to explore. I let go of the sheet and it joined the bedclothes on the floor. Cherie placed her palm between my breasts and pushed me onto the flat of my back. I felt incredibly exposed and erotic.

"Nice tits," she said, then drenched them with a warm sponge. I started. The sensation was wonderful, and her attentions so stern, so direct, nothing like Nicola's playfulness. She began circling my breasts with the damp sponge, sending maddening sensations along my body to pool between my legs. My nipples became rock hard, and she scrubbed at them as if she could wash them off my body. It didn't hurt, though. If anything, the brisk treatment turned me on even more.

Suddenly, she broke away and her sponge trailed down my belly to my navel. My abandoned breasts went stone cold and the chill became part of the eroticism. She circled my navel in larger and larger circles until my lower belly and top of my pubic hair was wet and awaiting the next pass of warmth. Cherie was driving me mad with hot and cold, wet and dry. She was a tease and she knew it.

The sponge descended farther, and she pushed it slowly between my legs. I moaned and opened wide for her, all thoughts of sex with Nicola fled to the back of my mind. I was hungry for this experience.

Cherie dragged the wet sponge back and forth across my clitoris. It was delicious, but there was not enough friction for me to come, and I so wanted to come. I raised my hips and Cherie stopped still.

"No way," she warned. "You move, even an inch, and it's over. Understand?"

I nodded furiously. What was it with nurses? Why were they all so bloody bossy? She began to rub me again. Her mouth closed around my left nipple and she sucked. I gasped. My nipples were definitely my weakness. My eyes flew open and I grabbed for her, wanting to sink my fingers in her short dark hair. She jerked away and suddenly I was freezing all over.

"Not the cap!" she snapped. "Don't you dare wreck my cap. If Debs comes on duty and I have *one hair* out of place, she'll hoist me by my knicker elastic."

"Okay, okay. Sorry." I clawed for her shoulders instead and brought her and her hand back into position. She clamped onto my left tit as if she wanted to draw the whole thing into her mouth. The sponge rasped against the tip of my clit, I was suspended on the brink of an orgasm for what felt like eternity. I was going to die, I just knew it. I'd have a heart attack and die right here on this bed.

Cherie must have sensed my dying wish, for she chucked the sponge in the washbowl and, with no warning, shoved two fingers inside me. I enveloped her fingers like cling film. I cemented myself around them, and still they pushed and pulled and plunged me over the edge into a skull-shattering orgasm. I was unaware of making any noise, but as I came down from my high-flying climax, her hand was sealed over my mouth and she was giggling uncontrollably.

"It's not right for noises like that to come out of an MRS." She giggled. "People will think we're amputating without anaesthetic."

"Was I loud?" I dragged in huge lungfuls of air.

"Sweetie, you were an opera."

My head spun. I'd been with two lovers in less than twelve hours. Oh, and I was gay. Yes, definitely gay. My feelings for Jackie, my old friend, slotted into place, and the aching wrench I felt by her dying made perfect sense. My feelings at this exact moment were more confusing. I was astounded. My body reeled with post-orgasmic aftershock, my brain was in a stupor, but I was elated, too. I, Penny Taylor, finally made sense of myself. It had been a long time coming, but I had finally arrived.

Chapter 7

Of course, my sheets were soaking, so Cherie moved me to another bed and stripped down my old one. I watched her as she worked—fast, efficient. Her body thrummed with something I recognised but was so out of place, I couldn't put my finger on it.

Cherie was clock-watching. She came over to me at a quarter to the hour and gave me a swift peck on the forehead.

"Okay, sweetie. I need to go finish off my paperwork before Debs arrives. I don't think I'll see you tomorrow, unless you can pull a miracle with Debs." She gave a lewd wink that only managed to confuse me.

To be honest, I'd have been happy to weigh anchor the next day, though it would hurt to leave behind all this good food. The more I was away from my platoon, the more anxious I became about missing training. I knew the career interviews were scheduled soon, and I needed to talk about the PTI course, since my whole reason for joining up was to become a physical instructor. Cherie peeled away and left with another wink. She seemed incredibly cheerful, and I was a wreck. I desperately wanted a nap and snuggled down to take it.

I'd barely shut my eyes, or so it seemed, when Cherie was back, this time with an older nurse. This had to be the Staff Nurse Doherty, or Debs, that she'd been going on about.

"Where's her chart?" Doherty frowned. She looked up, caught my eye, and held it for an uncomfortable minute. She was obviously schooled in malingerers, and I began to feel very shifty. Cherie looked about her, flushed and confused.

"Oh. Here it is." She plucked the clipboard off my original bed. We'd forgotten about it when we changed over beds. Her face was scarlet, so I assumed this was not a good end to her shift.

Doherty sniffed and scanned my report. "No meds?"

Cherie shook her head enthusiastically. "No. And he couldn't get out of here fast enough for the golf course, so I couldn't check with him either."

"Have you been in any discomfort, Private Taylor?" she asked me, obviously not approving of Cherie's openness about the MO's golfing habits.

I shook my head. "I feel great today, nurse."

"I see." Another sniff.

My notes were clipped to the end of my bed, and before anything else could be said, the phone rang while someone shouted simultaneously for attention at the front desk. Both nurses turned in wordless synchronicity and hot-footed it out of the ward.

This was interesting. I sat up and listened as keenly as I could to a lot of coming and going out front. Eventually, nosiness got the better of me and I went to the door and peeked along the corridor. A couple of ambulance drivers were wheeling a gurney straight for my ward. All I could make out were the soles of a pair of Gibson's women's parade shoes.

"Taylor! Get out of the way!" Staff Nurse Doherty ordered as she strutted beside the gurney. I stepped smartly aside and watched as they all sailed by. I didn't recognise the occupant. A young woman lay flat out cold. Cherie came in next and elbowed me sharply with a nod towards my bed. I leapt onto it and stayed out of the way, though I was all ears and eyes.

The two body snatchers, along with Doherty and Cherie, shared the load and together lifted the unconscious woman onto the bed diagonal from mine. Job done, the ambulance girls wheeled their gurney out.

"Call Doctor Fraser," Doherty instructed Cherie. "This

one will need a once-over for concussion." Cherie went off to call the doctor.

"What happened to her?" I leaned over on my elbow, all agog. She was in full dress uniform.

Doherty ignored me. "Private Worthing, and so we meet again." She addressed the unconscious lass as she consulted her notes, then tutted. "Fainted at parade practise." She may be ignoring me, but I got the impression the monologue was for my benefit and not the poor sprog flat out on the bed.

"Oh." I sat back against the pillows, surprised. Fainted? Surely, the best thing about the POP was finishing all this training crap and getting out of here. I'd be dancing the rumba, not passing out.

"Happens all the time." Doherty must have read my mind. "At least this one went tits up during practise and not the real thing. Every POP has a dropper. Worthing, here, is a nervous little thing. A country mouse born to a family of tigers."

"Huh?"

"She's always in MRS getting meds for her nerves. She hails from some highfalutin military family and she's rubbish. They should have sent her away to study the cello or something. Certainly not into the army. She's a complete waste of space here. All she's done is crumple my bed sheets since the moment she arrived."

I'd crumpled a few, too, but not in the way I imagined Worthing had.

"A dropper at every POP?" This was news and it fascinated me. *A POP drop, cool.*

"Mostly. It's rare if there isn't. Why do you think the medics are all over those parades?"

Cherie bounced back into the room with an update on Doctor Fraser. "He says he'll be fifteen minutes."

Doherty nodded. "You best be on your way, Wilson. Your shift ended half an hour ago."

"Yes, Staff Nurse Doherty." And without so much as a glance in my direction, the second greatest thing to ever happen to me—after Nicola—went out the door.

Fraser kept me in one more night and, at last, I caught up on my sleep under the stern eye of Debs Doherty.

I slept well, though my dreams were a jumble of body parts and longing, and I woke up confused about what had happened with Nicola and Cherie. I regretted none of it. In fact, I wanted more, but with Nicola. She was the one who'd grabbed my fancy first and she still did. Not to mention the jealousy I sensed from Cherie, and I decided that was something I should keep well away from. I wasn't daft. Except I was. Only a daft wanker would have had sex with both of them, under the circumstances. Apparently, I was the guy who couldn't keep it in his pants. When faced with possibility, I had chosen orgasms over good judgment.

In retrospect, I now knew what the betting had been about—sexual conquest. My frequent sojourns to the NAAFI bar had labelled me as fair game. I suppose that initial spike of recognition that had so intrigued me had worked both ways. My worry was, now that Nicola had won her bet, would she still be interested in me? And what would happen if she found out about Cherie? I had no idea how the nurses' games went, but hoped that Nicola had time for me later.

The next morning, I was sent on my way, resplendent with a decent breakfast and eager to see my mates again. I knew something was up the minute I hit my platoon floor on Block B. It was too quiet. Inside my room, I found Carol, Mandy, and Joan standing to attention beside their beds, a full kit laid out neatly on top of the covers.

"What's going on?" I hissed.

Carol nodded to my bed. "Get in uniform quick. Manners is doing a full inspection."

"We've laid out your kit for you," Joan said.

"Name tagged it and everything." Mandy glowed.

Sure enough, there were little cloth name tags sown into my kit and a flood of relief and kinship swamped me. My roomies had looked out for me in my absence. I wondered if they'd be so charitable if they knew I'd been shagging half of MRS instead of writhing in agony.

"Also, you missed the ID photographs," Mandy gushed in a giddy catch-up mode.

I dragged off my tracksuit. "Is that important?"

"You can probably fit it in with the new recruits in a week or two," Carol said. "Hurry, I can hear them coming up the stairs."

In the fastest change known to mankind, I was fully uniformed and at attention when Judy and Manners arrived on the top floor. They came in, glanced about, and left. Judy gave me a hard stare, her eyes wandering to the bed and my kit, tagged and laid out correctly. She left without a murmur. It was almost an anti-climax.

"Three Platoon, outside now!" Judy's order ricocheted down the corridor.

We grabbed our berets and legged it down the stairs. Once we'd fallen into squad, Manners came out and stood in front of us.

"Your kit wasn't too bad, but there is room for improvement, and understand, I fully expect to see improvement." She paced before us. "Two Coy's Passing Out Parade is tomorrow. Parents will be allowed on camp from 1300, and I want you to be on your *best* behaviour, wearing your *best* bib and tucker. Got that? Now, you have drill practice for the rest of this morning, and you lot need it, so let's get on with it."

I'd missed drill practice while I was ill, and I was anxious about making a mistake. The minute my feet hit the square, however, I was back in the rhythm of it. Unlike poor Worthing, probably still horizontal back at the MRS, I was a natural soldier, it seemed.

When we were dismissed, a few of us nipped off for a fag break.

"Has anyone seen a POP before?" Beryl, from Donna's room, asked. None of us had.

"I bet someone faints," I said, thinking of Worthing, and how Staff Nurse Doherty talked about droppers.

There was a moment of stunned silence. Then, "No!" People started speaking up. "Never!" The idea shocked them. It was an empathetic response. We couldn't think of anything worse.

"I bet it happens." I pushed on, thinking someone would take the bait. Donna rose like the big, daft guppy she was. She was always in my face.

"I'll take you on," she said with her familiar swagger. I loved that she was too stupid to know exactly how stupid she was. Her bet opened the floodgates, and everyone piled in and bet against me. *Don't let me down, Worthing.* I tried to hide my glee. If Worthing delivered, I'd be a couple of quid up, basically a week's wages for all my sins.

"Taylor. You missed your careers interview yesterday while you were lolling about in MRS, so I've made you a special appointment." Judy seemed disgruntled at having to do anything extracurricular for me. "Report to the education centre at 1400."

I'd also missed my ID photo being taken, but Judy must have forgotten about it. She was in such a foul mood, I wasn't going to remind her.

I was outside Major Greene's office by 1355. This was exciting. Now was my chance to be like one of those soldiers in the recruitment office posters. I'd reviewed my plan. If Ted Taylor wasn't going to help me through university towards a Physical Education diploma, then the army would. This was one of my main motivators for joining up. The other reason...well, I wasn't prepared to examine that just yet.

The door clicked opened at 1400 precisely. "Ah. Private Taylor. We meet at last." Major Greene gestured me into her office. "Come in and take a seat."

"Thank you, ma'am."

"I believe you were ill last week." She moved round behind her desk. "How are you feeling today?"

"Fine, thank you, ma'am."

"I see from your recruitment notes that Staff Sergeant Simms advised you to go for a commission," she stated bluntly, putting me on the back foot.

"Um, I didn't want to take that path, even though my father was a commissioned officer." I stumbled over my explanation. Why was that in my notes? Apparently, the army had a long memory and didn't like people having an opinion of their own. "Plus, I hadn't the educational qualifications," I added hastily. I didn't want the army pushing me back into a classroom to gain whatever qualifications were deemed necessary for a commission. I wanted to be a physical training instructor and nothing else would do.

Major Greene rustled through my papers. "Four GSEs." She sniffed, unimpressed.

"I'd like to try for the PTI board, ma'am," I said. This interview was not going the way I'd expected it to go. I was being boxed into a corner and wondered if Greene had a quota to fill somewhere else. "That was the career I was heading for on the outside, only I couldn't afford the university fees," I continued, deciding to play the honesty card. "It's why I signed up in the first place."

Her face was stone. So much for plaintive honesty. Perhaps I'd said the wrong thing?

"It's like this, Taylor," she said at last, after reading through my notes a second time. "The army doesn't like wasting the qualifications a soldier brings with her, which is what this PTI idea of yours will do. I already have you earmarked for the Intelligence Corps. To me, that's a good fit." She stared me straight in the eye.

I'd left behind a pen-pushing job at the engineering firm. I'd go mad behind a desk—I knew I would. I beat down the disappointment and gathered my courage.

"I'm sorry, ma'am, but if I can't be a PTI, then I don't want to do anything."

"You can't join the army and then 'do' nothing." A smile twitched the corners of her mouth. It gave me hope that there was a human under the uniform.

"Then I'll have to resign, ma'am," I said, standing. It was brash, but I had no other option. I was not sitting behind a desk if I could avoid it. I'd rather sweep the streets of Darlington.

"Sit down, Taylor," Major Greene ordered in exasperation. I sat down and waited while she flicked through my papers yet again. "I'm going to be honest with you,

Taylor," she finally said, sitting back in her chair and facing me fully while she laid out the facts. "There are only two places on the PTI board for this sitting and I hear Private Kent is a shoo-in. She's been training with the PTIs for several months now, so that only leaves one place." She paused, looking me over. "Do you honestly think you're good enough to secure that place?"

"Yes, ma'am, I do." I grabbed the chance with both hands and a mighty lie. I had no idea if I was good enough, but how was I ever going to find out unless I gave it all I had?

"And if you don't? What then?"

I blinked stupidly, my shiny little blob of hope blotted out by a bigger, darker conundrum.

"I think we can agree that if you fail the board, then you're heading for the Intelligence Corps. Correct, Taylor?"

"Yes, ma'am." So, there *was* a quota to fill, but I had stood my ground and been given a chance to find my own path outside of that. Luckily for me, Major Greene was one of the fairer officers. I left the careers office feeling exhilarated at having the chance to prove to Ted Taylor, Major Greene, and, in fact, the entire British Army, that they were wrong about me.

★ ★ ★

My luck kept its upturn the following afternoon. When the band struck up for 2Coy's Passing Out Parade, my skin tingled with the bass notes. This would be me in a few weeks. I stood with my colleagues, keeping one eye on Worthing—my little moneymaker—and the other on the medics. They were deployed along with an ambulance on the far side of the parade ground. Among them stood the body snatchers who had delivered Worthing to the MRS yesterday, along with Debs Doherty. But not Nicola. Nicola was the only person in the whole world I wanted to see. Then, she appeared, pushing through the crowd to stand beside Doherty, just as 2Coy marched onto the parade ground.

I made some excuses to my friends and wove my way through the crowds.

"Hi," I said as I approached. "I saw you from over there and thought I'd pop over to say hi." This was lame. Nicola gave me a quiet smile with a knowing twinkle in her eye, and my stomach fluttered.

"So," I went on gamely, "will I be seeing you around?" My stomach clenched tighter. Maybe it was the wrong thing to do with her Staff Sgt standing beside her?

"Maybe," she said, and didn't look put out at all. Then, "Maybe not." She really did enjoy torturing me. The twinkle gave it away.

Doherty was flitting glances around the parade ground. "You shouldn't be talking to us," she snapped.

"I just want to say thank you for looking after me," I answered.

"Hop to it," she said. "There's too many officers about."

Just then, Worthing went down like a ton of bricks, and, bless her, in the prescribed manner—face first and to attention. The army even had a rule on how to faint. No soldier in Her Majesty's Army was allowed to buckle at the knees. No, ma'am. If you were going down, you landed like a Canadian redwood, face down in the dirt and ramrod straight. Her family, sitting up on the bleachers, could at least be proud of how she followed orders.

Doherty and Nicola swooped in after the body snatchers, and I took the opportunity to melt away and collect my winnings.

That evening, for the first time, my entire Coy went to the NAAFI bar in force. The place was packed, now that 2Coy had been deployed and the newbies wouldn't arrive for another couple of weeks. Guildford went into relaxed mode. Everyone, except us, had a few weeks respite. And our Coy was pretty pleased at no longer being the bottom of the heap. So, everyone seemed to think they deserved a drink.

Nicola sat at a table with the other nurses. Cherie was also part of this medic gang. I knew better than to try and talk to Nicola, but I managed to send her a shy smile as I passed on the way to my table.

It wasn't long before Mandy started joking about the queers. There was a large group of the Q girls over in the opposite side of the room. How Mandy could know they were queer and why she never assumed that any other group, like the medics, hadn't any gays among them, was beyond me. I also wondered what my fellow recruits would have thought if they knew what I'd had been up to at the MRS.

"They're all freaks," Mandy said. "How can girls possibly sleep with each other?"

"How do you know that they're gay?" I asked, careful not to sound too defensive. "Have any of them ever come on to you or asked you to sleep with them?"

"No!" Mandy looked affronted. "But you can spot them a mile off." She sniffed. I could have thumped her. She was the most clueless, idiotic... "I wouldn't let one of them near me," she continued. "The thought of it makes me sick."

Some of the others, like Carol, Joan, and Mo, were clearly uncomfortable at Mandy's spitefulness.

"I'm sure you'll be totally safe," I said with mock reassurance, and placed my hand on her knee with an affectionate squeeze. I expected her to shriek and make fun of it, so we could all move on and clear the air. Instead, Mandy smiled back sweetly. I rolled my eyes. Typical of Mandy to miss the joke and do the queerest thing in the room.

Extracting myself, I went out to the loo and was surprised to find Cherie following me in. In fact, she followed me all the way into the cubicle.

"What are you doing?"

She made a grab for me, and I wriggled away.

"You're allowed off camp this weekend, fancy spending it with me?" she said.

This flustered me. If anyone was asking me out on my first free weekend, I wanted it to be Nicola. "I don't know, Cherie," I replied sheepishly. This was uncomfortable. "I haven't really thought about it."

Nearby, a door opened and closed. "We shouldn't be in here together," I whispered, my heart hammering.

"It happens all the time." Cherie gave me a cocky grin and reached for me again. This time I was more assertive and pushed back. I didn't want this risk. I wasn't prepared for it, and her attitude of ownership was raising my hackles. I felt too exposed stuck in this tiny cubicle.

"I don't want this," I said, plain and simple.

Her face soured. "You wanted it enough before."

"Well, this is now. I'm here with my mates, and all I want to do is have a pee. So, if you don't mind, could you please shift before we're caught?"

"Oh, don't you worry. I can do just that." And she stormed out, banging the metal door. My face flamed, but no one came to check out the noise. No one seemed to care.

Debs Doherty was the on-duty NCO that night. As was customary, she was dressed in her No2's uniform with the red sash and looked very dashing. She was waiting for me in the corridor between the toilets and the bar. She beckoned me outside and we stood sharing a fag on the NAAFI steps.

"Penny, I'm taking a risk here," she said between puffs.

"How?" I asked.

"You're not stupid. You must know something's going on over at MRS for Nicola and Cherie both to have sex with you, right?" She gave me a sharp sideways glance.

I toyed with the idea of looking confused, even shocked. Then, I gave in and shrugged.

"Sort of." I wasn't fooling myself, or anyone else. I'd guessed about the bet. They attempted to screw the new recruits and kept count. I had to admit, I had been a willing participant. It was sordid, but more fun than betting on two flies climbing a wall. That sharp edge I'd seen in Cherie and couldn't put my finger on was clear to me now. It was competition. She was as competitive as me, but I didn't see it when I was literally nose-to-nose with it. Cherie had known about Nicola and me, and had to draw level while I was in the MRS. So, why was she asking me out over this free weekend. Had they another bet?

"Betting aside," Debs said, "Cherie and Nicola both fancy you."

"What about you?" I asked cheekily. This conversation embarrassed me. It exposed me, so I slithered back into my familiar shell of wisecracks and irreverent behaviour. I was a lesbian. There was no doubt about that anymore, and I was glad. Here it was in the open, right before my eyes with no ceremony, whatsoever. Thanks to the nurses' game, the "lesliebiens" had gotten me, just as my mam had warned.

Debs snorted. "I'm not interested in anyone my nurses have fucked for a bet."

That cut. "Ouch."

Debs softened a little. "Dry yer eyes. It's just another competition between them. Cherie gets thick about things sometimes," she said. "Look, I'm up for promotion, and what I don't need is any bad feelings in my unit seeping out and polluting my prospects. Also, you're new here, but you should know by now to keep a low profile. If SIB sniffs anything funny, we're done for."

"SIB?" I'd never heard of it.

"Special Investigation Branch. They're part of the Military Police, and they spend an inordinate amount of time looking for queers."

"Oh." I didn't like the sound of that.

"What I'm saying is, keep your head down. And I don't care on who—Nicola or Cherie. But don't be stupid and play them off against each other and create waves, okay?"

"Of course, I won't. I'm not that daft." I was actually offended. Cherie was a player, but Nicola, for me, was something else. I had only the best of intentions toward her.

"That's why I shooed you away earlier at the parade. Any little misdemeanour can bring the spotlight on us. You're a recruit, so you're not meant to talk to us or be *friends* with the medics."

"Not even to say thank you?" I played the innocent.

It didn't wash with her. "Be careful is all I'm saying," she said, her voice hard with no-nonsense authority.

Several people came out of the bar and a few more were coming up the steps to enter. It had become busy. We needed to go. I ground my fag out under my shoe and said, perhaps a little too loudly, "Thanks for looking after me so well at the hospital the other night, Sergeant Doherty."

She turned and walked away. "It was our pleasure, Private Taylor," she called back.

Back inside, I was greeted by Nicola, who hovered near the slot machines by the main door. She was with a mate who was playing a machine—a pretty girl I recognised as one of the camp guards. She'd been on duty the day I arrived. Although she never once broke her rhythm tugging on the machine arm, she watched Nicola and me from the corner of her eye. How much did she know?

Nicola must have spotted Debs and me in conversation. She looked nervous.

"Everything all right?" I asked.

She gave me a hard, meaningful look and stalked off toward the bathrooms. I followed, intrigued and excited, not caring that the guard at the slot machine watched us depart.

"Who's that?" I asked as I followed her to the ladies'.

"Vicky. She's a mate. She's okay."

The toilet area was empty, and she grabbed me by the hand and dragged me into a stall. I began to realise toilet stalls would probably play a large part in any future romance. I went willingly and turned Nicola around into a passionate kiss.

This was different from my experience with Cherie in the stall opposite. I wanted this kiss. I pulled Nicola into my arms. Her hands meshed in my hair and the sweet scent of her perfume drove me wild. I began to unbutton her blouse, but she stilled my hands, dropping little kisses on my face and neck.

"Not here," she breathed. "It's not safe."

I found it hard not to continue exposing the creamy skin above her bra. I stroked the silkiness of her flesh and grinned as her nipples tightened under the cotton. It may have been dangerous, but she wanted me, too.

"What are you doing this weekend?" she asked. Her throat was flushed, a telltale sign that she was aroused.

"Nothing, except thinking of you. Why?" I couldn't care less about the weekend. I wanted to get Nicola so horny, she forgot where we were and let me touch her more. I trailed my fingertips down her stomach to her navel and her muscles quivered under my touch. This was different. We were on a level playing field, and I had a few tricks of my own to share.

"I have a friend who has a house near the camp. Fancy staying over with me?"

I hesitated in my explorations, immediately brightened by this idea. "I'd love that," I said. She took advantage of my hesitation to rearrange her clothing.

"What were you talking to Debs about?" she asked casually. My instinct was to lie. Nicola would not like it that Debs had exposed her feelings for me.

"She was giving me a heads up on SIB," I answered. Only half a lie, and it kept me on safe ground.

"You had sex with Cherie when I was off duty, didn't you?" This was more direct, and I was unsure how to deal with it, especially given Deb's warning. Plus, Nicola's eyes were slick with suspicion.

Oh, shit. I put on my best shocked expression. It was impossible to calculate how much she knew and how much the answer would hurt her. Would it be enough for her to know I wanted to be with her, and it was as simple as that? And, anyway, it was the medics' own stupid bet that had started all this deceit in the first place.

"I did have sex with Cherie," I found myself confessing. "I know it's no excuse, but she did come on strong, and before I knew it..." I stalled, lost for words, and guilt mixed with anger. "Wasn't that the bet, after all?" I challenged her back.

It was the right thing to do. Nicola's shoulders relaxed. She'd been testing me. So, she knew about Cherie.

"Do you like her?" Nicola was asking.

I shrugged. "I want to spend my first weekend off with you, don't I?" And that, thankfully, was an easy truth.

"I'm sorry about the bet, Penny," Nicola said. "I'm not playing anymore."

What did she mean? That she was through with the nurses' stupid game, that she wanted only me? I was about to question her when the toilets became busy with a lot of coming and going, and I realised I'd been away from my table for far too long and would have to answer questions.

"I'm glad you want to spend the weekend with me," Nicola said hurriedly, the commotion outside distracting her, too.

"Where will we meet?" I asked, waiting for an opportunity to open the door and escape back to the bar.

"Head down the Royal Mile, turn at the first right, then left. Sandy's house is number forty-seven."

It quietened down. Nicola cracked open the door, slipped out with a wink, and snipped the door shut behind her.

"But...but..." I was talking to a metal door. "What's the Royal Mile?"

I snuck back to my seat a minute later.

"Where were you?" Mandy pounced.

"Fighting off the queers in the loo. Don't go there, Mandy. They want you."

She sniffed and looked away, disgusted.

"Ever heard of the Royal Mile?" I asked my friends.
"Is it a pub?"

"Dunno." The question met with blank stares and shrugs.

"It's the road leading up to the camp. The one with all the bus stops." A girl—the guard who had let the bus pass on our first day—from the next table answered. Vicky was there with her.

"Oh, thanks." I gave her a friendly smile and was surprised at the beamer I got back.

"Are you going back home for the weekend, Penny?" Mandy asked. I already knew she was, and privately I thought she was crazy to make such a long journey on only a forty-eight-hour pass. "Say yes," she pleaded. "We can ride along together."

I shook my head. "I'm heading for London. I have an aunt there. It's all been arranged." The lie tripped easily off my tongue. I had a rendezvous with Nicola in a house on a nearby street, and I was determined to keep it. A team of wild horses couldn't stop me.

Chapter 8

We all left the NAAFI bar a little tipsy and giggled our way back to our block.

"Shush," Carol hissed once we reached our floor. Not everyone had gone out that night, and we would make no friends by waking people up. We tiptoed along the corridor to our room when the door opposite cracked open and Mo peeped out.

"Oh, thank God. It's only you lot." She sighed and swung the door open to reveal the other inhabitants of room one. They sat pale-faced and worried on the edges of their beds.

"What's going on?" I asked.

"We thought you were that bloody ghost," Mo said, shamefaced.

Intrigued, we piled in past her. "What about it?" Carol asked.

"Has it been here?" Mandy was already fretful.

"There's been all sorts of weird noises tonight," Doreen, Mo's roommate, said.

"What like?" I plonked myself on Mo's bed. As far as I was concerned, the night was still young, and the beer and my snog with Nicola had only served to wake me up. I didn't particularly want to go to bed, not when there was some good craic to be had across the landing. The others followed my lead, and we were soon camped out across the four beds in room one, ready for a gripping ghost story.

"Tell me about this ghost," Carol asked. "It's the first I've heard of it."

Mo wriggled in under her blankets, preparing to give us a tale. She was good at this sort of thing, a natural storyteller with an encyclopaedic memory for jokes and funny stories, and she could do all the voices, too. Mo was in her element, and we snuggled down, happy to be entertained.

"Someone in 2Coy told me that a recruit killed herself on this *very* floor ten years ago," Mo began in a hushed voice. "She hanged herself...in room...two!"

Mandy gave a squeak, and I clutched at her, winding her up even more.

Mo continued, "Her ghost forever regrets—"

"Why did she hang herself?" Joan, the practical one, asked. "I mean, it's not that bad here, is it?" She looked around for support. "And you can always opt out."

"Bet it was the food," I answered.

"Do you want to hear the story or not?" Mo looked miffed at the spotlight being snatched away.

"Go on, then."

Mo continued. "Her fiancé was a soldier who died in Korea—"

"That was more than ten years ago," Joan interrupted again. "She took her bleedin' time—"

"Shut up!" Mo shouted.

"Shush!" Carol held a finger to her lips. "Remember, the NCOs are just across the landing, and Judy has ears like a fruit bat."

"Anyway," Mo carried on begrudgingly, her voice regaining its spooky timbre. "She hanged herself for *whatever* reason, and sometimes at night, especially on a full moon," she pointed to the full moon outside the window, "you can hear her footsteps wandering along this corridor, looking for her room."

Mandy had gone pale and I couldn't resist, "I heard her bed was the first one on the right as you went in." This was Mandy's bed, and she glared daggers at me.

She clutched at Mo's arm. "It isn't, is it?" she asked.

Mo nodded solemnly, playing along. "I'm afraid it is, Mandy. One night you might feel the bedcovers lifting and a cold presence—"

Mandy leapt to her feet, ready to run all the way back to South Shields.

"Calm down," I soothed. "We're kidding you. It's really Joan's bed." There was an indignant squawk from Joan, and we all fell about, snorting with laughter.

"Shush," Carol said again, but she was laughing too, albeit quietly. Our laughter died away as we all became aware of a gentle tapping noise. It was hard to locate—it could have been inside the walls, or outside the window, or in the corridor. We fell into silence and listened. *Tap. Tap. Tap.*

Tap. Tap. Tap.

Everyone was looking at each other. "What's that?" Mandy finally asked, her voice thick with fright. We stared wide-eyed at each other.

Someone has to be taking the piss. But no one in the room was knocking on wood or playing silly games. The noise seemed to be all around us. Tap. Tap. Tap.

"It's the toes of her shoes," I said softly, feeling wicked, "tapping against the wall after she hanged herself."

Well, that was that. Mandy was on her feet and running for the door. At the same time, we all became aware of footsteps coming towards us at a measured, menacing pace. This only compounded Mandy's hysteria and our own self-inflicted fright. My jokey comment had backfired, and even I was frightened, as if I'd summoned the wraith with my disrespect. Mandy froze at the door as the footsteps stopped outside.

The doorknob slowly turned. Mandy shrieked and fell backwards across Mo's bed, landing on my lap. The door flung open and Judy stood on the threshold with a face like thunder.

"What's going on here!" she roared, without a care for those sleeping further down the corridor. Doors began to open, and heads popped out. "Well? Answer me, Turner!"

Mandy scrabbled off my knee babbling like a baby. "G-g-ghosts!" she finally managed to spit out.

"Ghosts!" A flicker of something like humour crossed Judy's face, but was gone in a flash. Her shoulders relaxed. "There are no ghosts." She actually spoke in a normal voice with normal volume. I was stunned. I didn't know she could do that.

"Every company tricks the newest recruits with ghost stories. It's nonsense and you're greener than pond scum to believe any of it." She stood back so we could file out. "Now get to your rooms before I run out of patience."

"But we heard tapping," Mandy snivelled. Right on cue, it started again.

Judy listened, then shook her head at our stupidity.

"That's the hot water pipes cooling down, you dipsticks." The volume was creeping back into her voice, her moment of humanity over.

We had to get out of there fast and hope she didn't smell drink off us. Meanwhile, the corridor was filling up with rubbernecks who, luckily for us, acted as a distraction for her ire.

"What are you lot gawping at? Back to your rooms, you pack of nosy buggers!"

There was enough scrambling and scrabbling for us to slip past Judy, duck into room two, and avoid any further ear-bashing.

The next day, the first minute I was free, I headed straight out to find Cpl Bury, who headed up the PTI training programme. I knew her by sight, and that her nickname was "Bones," as in "bury the bones." She'd never so much as looked in my direction and didn't seem very friendly.

"Is it as hard as everybody says?" I asked.

"Only the best get in," she said, bluntly. "I can't see you managing it, you've missed training and a week on my course equals a month on others. I'm not sure what Major Green was thinking, but you charmed her somehow." She gave me a sharp glance.

"I've only missed a couple of sessions." I was desperate for this chance.

"It's an upward trek from here. Are you still up for it?"

"You bet."

"Then, good luck. But you better be prepared to work bloody hard, Taylor. Otherwise, you're wasting everyone's time. I'm not cutting you any slack 'cause you're late in, got it?" With that, she turned her back on me and walked off. I was in! It was such a relief and I promised myself to break my own back to make this work.

Cpl Bury kept to her word that night and trained us hard. Because I'd been accepted to study Physical Education at Loughborough, I already had a good understanding of what would be involved. I even had previous teaching experience with the Guides and a few other volunteer groups, which I was able to put to good use, since it gave me a prior knowledge of all Bury's commands. I could see she was impressed—just a little. Bury was the down-to-earth sort who played no favourites. It was a boost for me, though. I felt less intimidated now that I had finally taken part in training.

The session did give me an overview of my biggest rival for the two places available. Sonya Kent was good. Very good. And she kept shooting me spiteful glances, so I surmised I was good too. Good enough to rattle her.

Private Kent had already been on the PTI course at Aldershot but had been RTU'd, or returned to unit, earlier in the year. Apparently, gaining a place wasn't insurance for an army career as a physical instructor. The PTI course was demanding and trainees were shed as the course progressed. Sonya had already been jettisoned once and had been kicking her heels in the guard room while she tried out for another coveted place. She swanned around as if she was a shoo-in. That put her in direct competition with me, though no way was she going to psyche me out. In fact, it made me buckle down and work harder, which was fine, since I had a lot of catching up to do.

If Sonya flunked this time, she was out for good. The fact that she'd already been through the grinder gave her a huge advantage over the rest of us for those two coveted positions. Unless she screwed up royally, one place would most likely go to her—and the other was mine!

On Saturday morning, our forty-eight-hour pass began. I was excited yet anxious, unsure what the weekend had in store for me. It was easy to sidestep my friends as everyone was in a tizzy to catch a bus or get to the train station and head home for the weekend. No one paid any attention as I packed a small bag and wandered happily toward the main gate and the Royal Mile beyond. I checked to see if Nicola's mate, Vicky, was on duty that morning. She wasn't. Another bored Regimental Policewoman watched me idle by.

It wasn't until I was actually out on the Royal Mile and saw the groups of girls milling around the bus stops that I realised this might not be as easy as I'd thought. What if someone saw me duck down a side street? There might be questions.

I carefully scoured the groups standing by the bus stops. So far, none of my platoon had appeared, but they could at any moment. It was now or never.

Nicola's instructions had been to turn first right and then left. I did as I was told and soon stood outside number forty-seven. It was a small terrace house with a balding lawn and a few straggly rose bushes. Lace curtains hung in the windows and the front door needed painting. It had a sad, unloved feel.

I began to lose faith. What if Nicola didn't like me after all? What if this was a setup between her and Cherie, and this house belonged to Judy's mother or something? Would they do that to me? Would Nicola be that cruel?

A sharp poke in the kidney made me jump. "Move your arse, Taylor. Stop loitering out here or we'll be seen."

It was Nicola. She swept past me and opened the door with her key. "Move it," she said and nodded for me to enter.

"Sandy," she called once we were in a narrow hallway with the door firmly closed behind us. "It's me."

"I'm in the back!" A shout came through from the kitchen. Nicola slung her coat over the stair rail and I did the same. I still had no clue what was going on. Leaving my bag at the foot of the stairs, I stayed glued to Nicola's heels as she moved through to the back parlour. It was furnished with a TV, sofa, and dining table. Everything looked worn and secondhand. A small, freckled woman came to greet us.

"Sandy, this is Penny," Nicola introduced us.

"Hi." I shyly shook her hand, aware I was being thoroughly appraised from head to toe.

"Where did you find this one, Nicola?" Sandy asked in a fruity tone that I didn't like.

"She's new to the camp. Met her in the MRS last week."

"I'm standing right here," I said, annoyed at being spoken of like this.

Sandy slapped my arm. "Welcome to my humble abode," she said and picked up a holdall from the sofa. "Have a fabulous time." I got a lewd wink.

She turned to Nicola, "I've left your groceries on the kitchen table. The milk is in the fridge and the bill is on the table under the ashtray. Toodle-pip, my lovers."

She shouldered her bag and left. Moments later, the front door slammed.

"Who's she?" I said, reminding Nicola she hadn't finished the introductions.

Nicola wandered into the kitchen and started putting away her shopping. "Sandy's an old army buddy of mine."

"She used to be in the army?" I was surprised.

"Yes. She was a medic like me. They chucked her out last year. She rents this house from another nurse who's been sent overseas."

"They chucked her out? What for?"

Nicola gave me a sharp look. "For being gay, of course. What do you think?" She paused in her unpacking. "Penny, you do know what you've let yourself in for?" There was genuine concern in her voice.

"Why rent a house around the corner from the base?" I was dumbstruck. It made no sense.

"'Cause all her friends are here." Nicola made it sound like the most natural thing in the world. "Plus, she lets us come around and be together, though we have to be careful. The MPs sometimes sit outside in unmarked cars to see if they can catch us."

This was a new world to me, and it made me uneasy. A cold lump solidified in the pit of my stomach. I'd always considered myself a rebel, but not enough to merit the attention of the military police. "Where's she going, then?" I asked, referring to the bag Sandy had with her. Did she bail out to give us privacy?

"Her girlfriend, Helen, is in Catterick. She's going up to see her." Catterick was in Yorkshire and the largest army garrison in Great Britain.

"Her girlfriend is in the army?" I was incredulous. This was weird.

"Yes." Nicola finished putting away the groceries and came around the table to wrap her arms around my waist. "They threw Sandy out 'cause she was a career soldier and reposted Helen to Catterick, 'cause she wanted out. That way they got at Sandy twice. No job, no girl. And it fucked over Helen, since she was unhappy and wanted to leave anyway. That's how it works in Her Majesty's forces."

"But why do that?" I was astounded at the pettiness of it.

Nicola shrugged. "'Cause they can. But Sandy had some money and rented this little house in an 'up yours' moment. So, at least the rest of us have somewhere to go. It's her way of giving Sybil the finger."

"Sybil. Is that like SIB?" They were the crowd Debs had warned me about.

"Yes. The Special Investigations Branch of the Military Police. SIB, but we call them Sybil. Their job is to weed out gays."

Debs hadn't been clear about how big a threat SIB could be. Throwing people out of the army, keeping unwilling people in, unmarked cars parked outside private houses? Now the actual threat was beginning to dawn on me. "How do they weed out the gays?" I was beginning to feel very naive.

"Snooping about. Sometimes they plant pretend gays in the camps to infiltrate us."

Pretend gays! "Jesus, that's a bit sneaky."

"They're dirt, but you have to play the game in order to stay safe, or else you'll get kicked out, or sent to Timbuktu."

"Does this mean we can't see each other again?" The reality hit me. Nicola and I had obstacles—nasty, career-shattering obstacles.

"We can, but we have to be very careful," she said. "This is the only pass you'll get while in training, so we'll have to sneak about inside camp."

"Is that how Sandy and Helen got caught? Are we going to be okay here?" I imagined the MPs kicking in the door.

"Yes." Nicola laughed. "Though I've had to jump over the back fence a time or two."

I wondered who she'd been here with, and a stab of jealousy hit me, alongside a stab of lust.

"It's safe enough," Nicola continued, "if you're careful." She shrugged. "It's all we've got."

Then, she grabbed my hand and dragged me towards the hall. "Now come upstairs. I've got plans for you."

Her plans included dressing herself up in sexy baby doll pyjamas. She made me get undressed and kneel on the bed, then did a sexy dance that had me grabbing for her. She'd flutter in close, then dance way again just out of reach. I waited patiently like a good girl and bided my time. Sure enough, she misjudged the distance and I lunged, dragging her screaming onto the bed with me. The lacy little thing didn't last long. I had it riding over her beautiful tits in no time. I ravished her breasts with my mouth while she fought with the lace caught over her face and hair. I held it there and took revenge for all the torture she had lavished on my tits in the MRS. I tweaked and sucked and nipped while she cried out and writhed in pretend horror.

Nicola had beautiful breasts. They were heavy and round with flat, pink nipples that quickly responded to any sensation. I blew on one and watched the pink bud ripen, shiny with my saliva. "Your tits stand to attention better than I do."

I moved down to her cunt. It was darker than her hair. Nicola was not a natural blonde. She had chemical means to get that platinum, baby blue-eyed look. I spread her legs and dived between them, spearing her with my tongue. At first, I plunged into her furiously. I was new to this, too eager and a little raw around the edges. Then I began to slow down, enjoying her taste and her soft whimpers. It was a natural thing. Her rhythm began to set the pace, and instinctively I sort of knew what to do, what she needed, and it was not fast and furious. I wanted to draw this out. It was our first legitimate time alone, a time to get to know each other's wants and desires. I kissed her cunt, my face slick with her want, and she ground down onto me, not hard but soft and slow. Nicola didn't need pressure, I realised. Like her nipples, her sex responded to light stimulation. Was there a connection? I couldn't remember what Cherie's tits were like.

This was a revelation, and I pulled back and began to actually explore her. Her clitoris was small and with the hood fully pulled back, it glistened like a little pearl. Her labia was ruby red and opened shyly for me. She was so very ready, and when I brushed her with my fingertips, she moaned and her labia quivered. I dipped my index finger into her and she squirmed, so I added another and began to fuck her, but not hard. She went wild, and I stopped, holding my fingers still inside her. The walls of her cunt flexed against them.

"Stop torturing me," she murmured.

"I think you'll find you're the one who started it with your little dance." I pulled my fingers out and blew on her clit. My fingers were slick with her, and I traced them idly round to her little pink anus. It scrunched up like a cat's arse as I tickled it. She squirmed again, but not in an unhappy way—she was just a little embarrassed.

"Do you like that?" I asked.

"It's okay. Not really my thing."

I pressed a little harder and she opened up for me. "Not your thing?"

My answer was a moan. A very sexy moan. I lowered my mouth to her clit and sucked, pushing my finger into her ass as far as it would go. It was as if I'd burst out of the rodeo stalls, riding a bucking bronco. She went crazy. She grabbed my hair so hard I thought she'd pull it out by the roots. I held on, my mouth sucking her with all my strength, flicking her clit with the tip of my tongue, strumming it, while my finger pistoned her tight little ass. She rolled her hips, gave a loud scream, and then collapsed in a sweaty mess.

"Oh, my God." She pushed her hair out of her eyes. "That was fantastic."

"I think you broke my finger." I laughed.

"Oh, come here, you." She gathered me up in a big hug and dropped kisses all over my face until we were both laughing.

"If SIB's outside, they'll know exactly what's going on in here with you screaming like that," I said, a little proud she had enjoyed it so much.

"They're all pervs, anyway. I bet they'd get a thrill out of it."

"Let me go. I need to pee." I squirmed out from under her and ran to wash up in the bathroom.

We snuggled down and cuddled for a while until she got her breath back. "You're a good lover," she said, playing with my hands. "Look at the length of your fingers!"

I nuzzled her neck, wanting her to recover quicker. I was ready for round two. "And every one of them is for you," I said.

"Was I really your first? Back in the MRS."

"Well, somebody had to be." I laughed. "Unless you count a few kisses." Her hands stilled, and she stopped playing with my fingers.

"Oh, sweetie. I feel so bad. I'd have made it nicer if I'd known."

I laughed even harder. "It was just fine as it was, silly." I rolled her over and kissed her mouth, long and slow. "Look at what you did. I'm insatiable." I drew back to look adoringly at her.

"Well, you're a fast learner, that's all I can say."

"I'm a natural." I sighed in contentment and kissed her again.

Nicola kissed my face and my throat, then worked her way with her tongue all down my body until she hovered over my cunt. Then she lowered her head and began to slowly lick the length of me. It was delicious. Her tongue was so sweet and soft, and she gently strummed me to climax. It wasn't as raucous as her orgasm, but it was exactly what I needed.

"Are you hungry?" I asked after a long snuggle.

She thought about it. "Maybe a little."

"How about I make us an omelette, and we can eat it in bed?" I made a killer omelette and wanted to show off for her. Besides, sex made me hungry—another new discovery.

I pulled on my tee shirt and knickers. Nicola borrowed Sandy's dressing gown and joined me in the kitchen.

"Who was she?" she asked, while I cracked eggs into a bowl.

"Who? Pass me that whisk, please."

"You said you'd kissed someone before."

"Jackie," I said, and a tiny flutter of sadness played across my heart. "She died in a motorcycle accident earlier this year." Our relationship had been so innocent compared to what I knew now. Poor Jackie. Like me, she'd struggled to escape the confines of our hometown. It was Jackie who'd sparked my imagination with her dreams of travel and adventure, and now she was buried in the local cemetery, stuck in stupid Darlington forever. I'd been so lonely when she'd died. I'd felt panicked and trapped without her vision to help me break out.

"Oh. I'm sorry." Nicola rubbed my shoulders. "Were you close?"

The questions were upsetting. I didn't want to go down that old road, not today with so many new roads opening up to me. "Close enough to make everything different after she was gone."

"But how did—"

"How about you make a pot of tea," I interrupted her.

A shadow flitted over her eyes. It was hard to read. Was she mad at me for not wanting to talk about Jackie? For shutting her out?

She filled the kettle. "I didn't mean to be nosy," she said defensively. "It's just hard to believe all you did was kiss. You seem so...natural in bed."

"Well, it feels natural with you," I said, but I felt a flutter of anxiety. Jealousy. That's what I'd seen in her face. How could she be jealous of a dead girl? I decided to cajole her out of her mood. The omelette was looking after itself for the next few minutes and the kettle was bubbling on the stove top. I came up behind her and put my arms around her.

"I can't believe you've been with just one girl," she said again, but it was not accusatory.

"Maybe you bring out the best in me?"

"Cherie said it, too."

Ah, Cherie. Here comes the trouble Debs warned me about. "What did she say?"

"That you were a right ride."

Put bluntly like that it didn't sound very complimentary. "Well, remember, I chose to be with you this weekend and not her. She's probably got a dose of sour grapes."

Nicola turned in my arms and snuggled in. "I think I've created a monster," she joked. "I think if you had the chance, you'd chase after half the camp."

"I don't want half the camp. I want you." Why was this such hard work? We'd only just met. This weekend was supposed to be all about sex, not navel-gazing. The kettle began to whistle, and I left her to her tea making and went back to my omelette.

We had our lunch in bed, followed by more sex and then a bath. We spent the rest of the weekend eating and fucking and, thankfully, not really talking about anything deep again. Nicola sometimes went off into quiet little moods, and I snatched a snooze at those times. And then, it was Sunday afternoon and Sandy was due back. We had to tidy the house and somehow get out of it unnoticed.

"You leave first and I'll follow after in about ten minutes."

"But why?"

Nicola sighed. "Have you forgotten all I told you about being careful? Sometimes SIB follows Sandy, so they'll know she's been to Catterick this weekend. If they follow her back here, and you're seen coming out the door..."

"Ah." It was sad to see the machinations ahead of me, perhaps for my entire army career. I grabbed my bag, and with a quick peck on Nicola's lips, left first.

The Royal Mile seemed longer than ever, but I had a lot on my mind and probably a slower step while I digested everything that had happened that weekend.

Nicola was a possessive lover, and I wasn't sure I liked or wanted that. Especially in the rarefied, spied-on culture of army gay life. Simply put, I was in Guildford for a short time, I had just come out, and I wanted sex. The truth was, now that I'd discovered sex, and apparently was a natural at it, I didn't want to stop.

The RP on guard at the main gate was Vicky, the pretty blonde girl I'd seen earlier, and I quickened my step towards her, casting my mind about furiously for something witty to say.

"Has anyone tried to escape yet?" It wasn't much as far as witticisms go, but she smiled kindly at me.

"Not that I've noticed," she said. "And I wouldn't care if they did." Her blonde hair was naturally curly and her front teeth slightly crooked, which gave her a cheeky, sexy sort of smile. "Are you in training?"

"Yes," I answered a little too eagerly. My face coloured and I felt gauche.

"Haven't I seen you in the NAAFI bar?" It seemed she was happy to chat. Maybe guard duty was as boring as it looked.

"Yes. I've been there a few times, if I can dodge Judy," I said.

"Judy?"

"Corporal Hacker. We call her Judy after the Punch and Judy puppet."

The guard snorted. "I can see you're taking your training seriously. You'll go far in the army."

I wasn't sure if she was being sarcastic, so I just grinned.

"Did you have a nice weekend?" she asked next. She was stretching out the conversation, which had to be a good sign. Unless she was bored out of her mind, and talking to any nob was better than this naff job.

"Oh, yes," I said brightly, my confidence flooding back. "I went to my see my auntie in London. Aunt Sibyl." It was mischief making and I watched her closely for clues. Was she one of us?

Vicky blinked and started in surprise, and I got my answer. Vicky was family.

"You're a cheeky sod, Taylor." She laughed.

I said farewell and went on my way with a jaunty whistle.

Chapter 9

As a result of the freedom of the weekend, Monday morning was my first real low. My body buzzed every time I thought of Nicola and the things we'd got up to. I kept an eye out for her everywhere I went, wondering if I could feign another illness and spend some time with her. I was confused—part of me ached for her, and another part warned me that she would be an uncompromising lover. Simply put, a relationship with Nicola was a case of all or nothing. Then, I remembered the warnings I'd received and decided not to push it. In the army, there could never be an "all," nor would there ever be a "nothing," only a fine line between the two. I didn't want SIB knocking on my door. Sandy and Helen's story cooled my ardour.

My bad, sad, and confused mood was with me the next morning. It was a drill morning, too, so I could lose my bitter thoughts in square bashing. However, while I could march blindfolded by now, having a sort of natural rhythm, a lot of my fellow "toonies" couldn't. In fact, several of them were woeful. It was as if their brains didn't talk to any body part lower than their knees.

"We're never going to win a cup," Carol muttered to me. We were standing at ease to the side as Cpl Evans marched 4Plat, her platoon, off for their tea break. "Not against that lot." Carol twitched her head slightly at the passing 4Plat. "They're super good."

"I told you before, listen to how she does her instructions." We both shut up and listened to Evans's Welsh singsong lilt as her platoon disappeared around the corner. "She croons them into being that bloody good," I concluded. "She sneaks the marching rhythm into them with her Welsh lullaby voice."

"Christ, I think you're right."

"You can ask Christ all you like. I *am* right, and he's only going to agree with me," I muttered through clenched teeth, staring straight ahead.

"I'm surprised your head fits a regulation beret."

I chuckled, and then we all solemnly hushed as 1Plat passed by. Like us, they were a pack of unlucky buggers with the training NCO they'd pulled. Judy was bad, but she wasn't the only crappy corporal. The army owned the patent for angry, frustrated spinsters and threw them straight at its recruits.

One Plat had Cpl Meeke, who was in no way whatsoever like her name. She was a harridan, as broad as she was tall. A big, angry woman with the delivery of a foghorn. She'd barraged 1Plat into a shivering pack of jellyfish, and inflicted damage that was never going to be reversed. Basically, they were fucked as far as the recruits' competition went. And while I felt sorry for them, I was also glad a quarter of the competition was sucking their thumbs at night while bed-wetting.

One Plat were atrocious at parade drill. I'd have no takers on someone fainting at our own Passing Out Parade. Each and every one of 1Plat would be face down in the dirt in under a minute. Rumour had it air mattresses had been ordered in for them.

"Look at me," Meeke screamed at her lot. "When I say to the right, go right. Nowhere else but the right. Get it?"

One poor bastard hesitated a fraction of a second too long. There was a collective drawn breath from 3Plat, lined up by the edge of the square.

"Armstrong, you duffer. You do as I say, when I say. I don't care if your knickers hit your ankles, you march!"

Poor Armstrong. She was a shy girl with a mild stutter, and she had all our sympathy as 1Plat limped off the square, slump-shouldered and utterly defeated. Yep, one platoon down, two to go.

"**I**'ve been thinking, Penny." Carol pulled my attention anyway from my military law book. It was nearly 2100 hours. We had a test coming up Monday morning and I was worried. I always struggled with this subject. All four of us were on our beds, three of us swotting over one subject or another. Mandy, as unconcerned as ever, read a magazine in her pyjamas.

"Thinking what?" I asked.

"Everyone can lift a book and cram." She waved her *Map Reading and Orientation* book. Carol was smart and a natural swot. She was reading her book for pleasure, I was sure of it. "But with the drill, we're stuffed. What we need is a little more practice, and I'm sure the worst of us could crack it."

"Even more drill?" Mandy pulled a face. She was okay at it, but hated it.

"Not for you. You don't need it." Joan pointed at her. "But someone like Doreen, for instance. She's great at everything except drill. She's got two left feet. And Beryl isn't far behind her."

"Elaine is no twinkle toes either," I mused, mulling over Carol's words. There was a kernel of a good idea in there. In fact, it made bloody good sense. "We could use the hockey pitch after tea. It's down a slope and we'd be fairly private. Who would be the drill sergeant, though?"

Carol threw her *Map Reading and Orientation* at me. "You, you big nana!"

The next time I saw Nicola, she was sitting at the cookhouse with Vicky and a nurse whose name I didn't know. The table nearest them was vacant, so I made a beeline for it. Nicola saw me approach and scowled at me.

"...and she said she was staying with her Auntie Sibyl." Vicky and the other girl howled with laughter, and that's when I realised they'd been talking about me. Nicola must have kicked them under the table because they shut up sharpish.

"Excuse me," I called over, "have you any salt?" I rattled the empty saltcellar from my table. I met Nicola's gaze and smiled, all sweetness and light. I loved teasing her a little.

"Here, cheeky." Vicky thumped their full one down on my table.

I gave her a grin worthy of a cheeky woman and Vicky smiled back. When I looked up, Nicola's scowl was even fiercer. By then, Mo and Carol had joined me, and Mandy was on her way with her food tray. I decided to ignore the table to my right, along with Nicola's scowling, and talk to my mates instead. I wasn't sure what was going on with Nicola. I found her whole hot-cold act confusing.

In the cookhouse, empty food trays had to be taken to a special trolley by the waste bins. Leftover food went into the bins and the trays then slid onto the trolley. When I took mine over, Nicola was loitering, taking time dumping her leftovers into a bin.

"I hear you and Vicky had a right laugh," she said by way of greeting.

"It was just a joke on the way back in." I was surprised at her chosen topic. We had about three seconds before someone else descended on the trolley station and she wanted to talk about Vicky?

"I saw the way you looked at each other just now. You fancy her, don't you?"

"Oh, for Christ's sake. It's you I want."

"I'm not so sure of that anymore."

"Well, it is. When can I see you again?" People were already heading our way. "Please?"

She sniffed, but aware our time was ending, concluded the theatrics and said, "I'm on nights. Come over after eight thirty."

Most nights were spent at the NAAFI, now that my platoon wasn't so shy about using it anymore. That night, rooms one and two, my main muckers, convened at the bar to dream up our own ghost story for the new recruits, who were arriving any day now. It was a corker. The best one ever. We weren't going for anything as lame as a ghost story. We were going to make our very own ghost!

We'd make a phantom out of a uniform jacket and forage cap, a broom, a mop for the head, and coat hangers, and fly it on a rig past the new sprogs' windows. We howled with laughter, imagining the knicker-wetting that would ensue. The evening passed with pen, paper, and precision planning. Sgt Manners would have been proud of how we engineered our ghost, delegated everyone's role, and made it all come together seamlessly—at least on paper. I was in fine fettle, looking forward to my rendezvous with Nicola later. I'd go back to the dorms with the others, then feign a headache and nip out for aspirin. Job done, we headed merrily back to Block B, where we bumped into Beryl Stewart on the top stairwell. She looked flustered.

"What's up?" I asked.

"Donna's put her back out."

"Oh, no." Donna out of whack? I had to see this, even if I was a few minutes late for Nicola. "Dearie me. Let's go, gang."

We were on a high of beer and planning the best practical joke this camp had ever seen. We'd be legends. We piled up the stairs into Donna's room. Sure enough, she lay flat on her back in bed, wearing an exaggerated grimace on her face.

"Are you all right, duck?" I asked, all concern and kindness.

"I can't move," she said through clenched teeth.

"Not even to get out of bed?" I asked sweetly.

"No," she grunted.

"Right, then." I slapped my hands together. "We need to get this mattress on the floor. My mam used to put her back out and sleeping on the floor always helped."

"Yeah," agreed Joan. "These beds are crap. The springs are gone."

"No. No. Don't move me," Donna hissed. "Don't—"

But in our drunken camaraderie, we had her lifted on high, then dumped on the floor in no time.

"There now. Isn't that better?" I asked, not giving much of a damn either way. Donna was a snitch and it was good to get my own back.

"What's going on here?" Judy appeared behind us as if by magic. I began to wonder if she had hidden cameras in all the rooms.

"Donna has a bad back, Corporal." Beryl spoke up for her roommate.

"And how does sprawling her all over the floor and wrecking her bed improve things?" Judy snapped. "Did it occur to you to come to me, Private Stewart?"

"It did, Corporal," Beryl babbled. "I was just on my way when I met..." She trailed off when she realised what she was saying. Judy's eyes narrowed and focused on me. My karma was so spot on.

"...when you met this lot." She as good as snarled. She was in foul form tonight. "Get back to your rooms, all of you. Stewart, go get the medics."

We got to our various rooms, glad to be out of Judy's sight. The next quarter of an hour was filled with much coming and going in Donna's room. My stomach sank. There'd be no nipping out for aspirin for me tonight. I hoped Nicola would understand. Suddenly, Donna's wellbeing took precedent, and the karmic lesson learned.

We prepared for bed and decided to forgo ablutions until the furore next door died down. No point in being a moving target and drawing further fire from Judy. Luckily, I'd used the loo at the NAAFI before we'd set out for home. Mandy hadn't and was dancing from foot to foot.

"What do you think they're doing out there?" she asked.

"Dunno." I slid into bed, disinterested.

"I need to go to the loo." Mandy jiggled a little bit more.

"Then go."

"Shut up, you two, or we'll have her landing in on us," Carol warned.

Mandy dragged a chair over to the door and stood on it on tiptoes to peer out the glass panel at the top. "I can see some medics," she said. "They've got the body snatchers and a stretcher."

"Who is it?" I asked, resisting the urge to push Mandy off her chair and leap up to see if Nicola was in attendance.

"It's Donna," she answered, looking at me confused.

"Of course it's bloody Donna. She's the one with the busted back!" Sometimes Mandy was thicker than burnt jam.

"You two need to shut up," Joan hissed. Her advice was right, but too late. The door burst open and whacked against Mandy's chair, sending her toppling backward onto her bed. Judy appeared on the threshold, her face red with anger.

"If you lot don't shut it and get to sleep, I'll have you doing drill all day tomorrow until your legs are bleeding stumps. Do you hear me?"

People in Block D had probably heard her. The patrons at the NAAFI bar had probably heard her. Maybe Sandy down on Royal Mile had heard...that's when I realised she was glaring at me, even though it was Mandy who was sprawled out on her bed like a slab of road kill.

"There's a recruit lying injured next door, thanks to the stupidity of someone moving her without authorisation!"

Oh. That's why I was getting the glare and not Mandy. I wondered if Donna was seriously injured or just hamming it up. She was bitchy enough to relish getting me shafted for "helping" her. If anything was wrong with Donna, it had to be faecal poisoning from all the brown-nosing she did.

"Yes, Corporal," we mumbled from behind our bedsheets. Judy gave us another heated glare, then someone outside asked a question and stole her attention. She slammed the door in our faces and returned to the drama next door.

"I nearly wet myself." Mandy laughed as soon as the door was shut. She found it tremendously amusing, but then again, she had not been the target of Judy's wrath. I had and, therefore, was in no mood for Mandy's chortles.

"Shut up or she'll be back, and we all know who she'll blame," I said.

"Ooh. Now I really need to go." Mandy was up, beginning her wiggle dance again.

"Seriously, shut up!" Carol was becoming angry. I thought her anger was directed at me, so I defended myself, still stinging from the accusation that *I* had somehow dislocated Donna's stupid back. How had she passed the entrance medical examination anyway?

"It's her. She's the one blabbing on." I blamed Mandy in an angry hiss. Then, "What the hell?" Mandy stood by the wall with a glass in her hand, trying to listen to the conversation next door. "What are you doing?" I asked in disbelief.

"Eavesdropping."

"Just go to the ablutions, Mandy," Carol said, wearily. "No one will say anything to you."

"No one else has gone yet and I don't want to be the first," Mandy said in her whining voice, the one that irritated us all. "Come with me, Penny."

"No. I don't need to go." I rolled over in bed, turning my back to her. No way was I exposing my face to Judy again. I wanted to keep it attached to my skull.

"I can't hear a word," Mandy piped up a few moments later. We could all hear the rumble of voices through the wall, though not the actual words. Mandy was just being nosy.

"That's 'cause it's a plastic glass beaker," I mumbled, teetering on the edge of sleep. "You need a glass glass."

"Have we any glass glasses?"

I sighed, my drowsiness receding as my irritation grew. "No. Only the water jug is glass."

"Great." Mandy skipped over to the windowsill with the water jug sitting on it. I caught Carol's glance of sufferance and rolled my eyes. Mandy was a right twit when she went into giddy mode. Having a few beers only exacerbated it.

"It's full of water." The next instalment of Mandy's woes began.

"Shut up," Joan snapped.

"For God's sake, go to bed." Carol's rebuke was much milder than mine.

"Pee in the bloody jug if you're that desperate."

"I'm *not* going to pee in the water jug." Mandy was highly offended. "I want to use it to listen at the wall."

"Then throw the water out and get on with it. And let us get to sleep," I snapped, all patience gone.

Mandy's moods often flipped from giddy to peevish when she tried people's patience too far. She wouldn't talk back to anyone. Instead, she would show her displeasure in childish ways, especially if she'd had a few bevvies. Tonight she threw the window open with a mighty bang that brought us all bolt upright in our beds.

"For God's sake, Mandy!" We were horrified. Judy would be back in an instant.

Except she wasn't.

With a smug smile, Mandy locked eyes with me and casually tipped the contents of the jug out the window. "I *am* going to pee in it!" she announced.

Her crowing was cut short by an angry squawk from below. Mandy went white. She peeped out the window and withdrew immediately, slamming it closed.

She turned to us in panic. "I just tipped water all over Judy."

"You're dead." I put it succinctly, though my heart was pounding.

"Mandy, we hardly knew ye," Joan sang. There was spite in her singsong words and I swear we were all feeling a malicious triumph over Mandy at that moment. She had pushed and pushed and would get what she deserved. Judy had obviously looked out her office window to see what the banging was about and got a face full of water from above. Mandy would be the minced meat in tomorrow's cottage pie at the officers' mess.

Already we could hear footsteps thundering toward us. It could only be Judy torpedoing straight for us. My stomach cramped and Mandy looked hysterical. She jumped into bed fully clothed and pulled the covers up to her ears. The door exploded open. For a moment, I wondered if Judy had kicked it in. I slunk down in my bed as deep as I could go, like a child in a thunderstorm.

"*You*, Turner, and *you*, Taylor," she bellowed. "Of all the—"

"But—" I began.

"Shut it! I don't care what you have to say, Taylor. If there's any aggro going down, you're in the thick of it." She was apoplectic. Her face was purple. At any moment, she'd hit the floor with a burst blood vessel. *And we all know who'd get the blame for that.*

"I will see you both at 0800 hours in my office. Get it?" she roared.

"Yes, Corporal," we bleated, like lambs for slaughter. She stormed out as quietly as she'd stormed in. The whole floor was so silent you could hear a pin drop in every room along the corridor. She'd turned the entire block rigid with fright.

"Mandy," I whispered.

"Yes," she whispered back.

"If we get handed our papers tomorrow morning, I'm going to take you out to that parade ground and give you the biggest kicking of your life. Get it?" I hissed the last part as loud as I dared.

There was no answer, only the rustle of Mandy's bed-clothes and, soon after that, sniffling as she cried herself to sleep under the covers.

The next morning at 0800, we were standing to attention in Hacker's office. She did her usual trick of ignoring us for five minutes, which seemed to stretch to five years.

Finally, she looked up and rested back in her chair. "I've thought long and hard about you two." She sounded almost cheerful, which I took to be a bad sign. Beside me, Mandy relaxed, but then, she was a tithead and knew no better.

"The parade ground looks dusty," Judy said.

Of course it did. A parade ground is in the open air in constant use—I went cold. *Oh, no. She's not going to...* I could see what was coming next.

"There are your brushes." Judy indicated two sets of hand brushes and dustpans by the door. "Collect them and get out."

"You want us to sweep the parade square with hand brushes?" I asked to make sure I understood this idiocy correctly.

"Yes." Judy gave a beatific smile. "You start at 1800 hours, and if you don't finish it tonight, then you continue tomorrow night until it's done. Understand?" She raised her eyebrows sweetly.

I did understand. *Bitch, bitch, bitch.*

We spent two nights brushing down the parade square. Meaning, I missed a training night for the PTI board and didn't get to see Nicola, not even to apologise for the previous no-show. By the time we'd finished, I had a backache, a hand full of blisters, and a very poor relationship with Mandy.

The daily routine was familiar to me now, and I got through the drills and gym classes easily. Less fun were the English and math lessons, and most boring of all, the military law and protocol classes that the army rammed down our throats every bloody day. The week trudged along on hobnailed boots.

They had given us Friday afternoon off. I planned to spend the afternoon getting my kit ready for the big church parade on Sunday. Another thing not to look forward to.

On returning to our block after lunch, we noticed sheets and blankets hanging out of our room windows.

"What the hell has gone off?" We rushed to our floor to find our entire floor ransacked. Every room had suffered the same fate. Drawers had been pulled open and the contents tipped onto the floor, mattresses had been pulled off the bed frames, and bed linens were strewn everywhere, even hanging out the windows. Our block looked as if a tornado had hit.

"What the fuck?"

"It has to be Judy." I was furious. Our afternoon off had been scuppered by malicious pettiness.

LCpl Adams hollered down the corridor, "Three Plat to platoon office now!"

Sgt Manners was at her desk when we came in.

"I inspected your rooms this morning and found the worst pig sty I've ever seen in my entire life."

Yeah, like you'd know a pig sty up close and personal. Luckily, I managed to bite my tongue.

"The beds looked like tramps had slept in them," she continued. "On Monday night, there will be another inspection and I better not find so much as a speck of dust. Got that?"

We made the mistake of taking a breath before answering in unison. It wasn't quick enough.

"Got that?"

"Yes, Sergeant Manners." We were faster this time. I assumed we'd be dismissed, but Manners suddenly went maudlin. Never a good sign. She wandered over to profile herself against the window like something out of a B movie.

"Three Plat is going to win the Accommodation Cup next week, even if it kills you trying," she began. Then she spun to face us and said, "Sunday is your church parade. Assemble outside the block at 0930. We'll march to the parade square for OC's inspection, then we march as a company to the church."

"Excuse me, Sergeant," Elaine bravely spoke up, "but I'm a Quaker. Do I have to attend the ceremony?"

"Anyone who can't attend for religious reasons will stand to attention outside the church until the ceremony is over."

"Excuse me, Sergeant." I tried next. "I'm an atheist—"

"Is that what it says on your record, Taylor," she snapped.

I had to think about what I'd said to Simms all those months ago. "Um. I think it says Methodist, but—"

"Then Methodist you are."

I shut up.

Manners wound up our little interview. "Although your rooms were disgraceful, I've decided to be kind and to still allow you the rest of the afternoon off—after you tidy your rooms, of course. Now, get out of my office."

"She wants to win that Accommodation Cup so badly, but we're the ones who will hurt," I said, as we stomped back upstairs to begin rearranging our rooms.

"Our rooms were okay," Carol complained.

"She was making a point in her own special way," said Joan.

"Has anyone seen my other shoe?" Mo came out of her room holding up one platform boot, part of her civilian clothing.

"Ask Frankenstein." I eyed the six-inch wedge heel.

"You're all so bloody funny," Mo groused. "I can't find any of my stuff."

"Here it is, in my room." Bridget tossed the boot over.

"Dear God, she's even tossed things across the rooms." I was gobsmacked by the wanton carnage. "We better win this cup, 'cause I don't want to face her if we lose."

"She didn't have to wreck our rooms," Doreen said. "A little bit of encouragement would have done wonders." She teetered under a pile of reclaimed bed linen, looking more like a hospital orderly than a soldier.

"At least she emptied our drawers for us." Carol always made us see the positive side. "All we've got to do is dust the insides and replace everything tidily."

"Good point," I said. "Let's get to it."

"Who's the best platoon?" Joan roared down the corridor.

"We are!" We roared back.

After 2Coy shipped out, a weird calm had descended on the camp. The training staff had a fortnight's rest before the next batch of recruits arrived. Everyone was relaxed, restful, and then—just like that—it began all over again. The next batch arrived. Sure enough, when they eventually came, they came in their busloads.

Mid-morning, on the fourth Monday of our stay, the first of several buses drew up and disgorged a gaggle of girls in civilian clothes. *Jesus, did I look that green on my first day?*

The new recruits had arrived and the cycle began all over again. We in 1Coy had advanced a step closer from being the camp sprogs to real soldiers. The old 2Coy had already been deployed, so these girls would be the new 2Coy, divided up alphabetically into platoons, as we had been. We were only a few weeks ahead training-wise, but watching them mill around awestruck outside the accommodation blocks made us feel a million years more advanced.

Chapter 10

The morning dragged with drill, inspection, military law class, and lunch. The afternoon looked little better, with even more classes.

I was alone, heading to the cookhouse around lunchtime and in no particular hurry to catch up with the rest of my platoon, when I saw her. Well, her back. But I'd know the manner of her walk anywhere. The sway of her shoulders, the tilt of her head, even the way her hair brushed against her uniform collar.

"Nicola," I called and went to follow. She kept on walking, and I had the feeling she'd seen me first and had turned away. Her stride was too long, too fast. This made me angry, and I broke into a jog, then a full-fledged run. I caught up with her and grabbed her by the elbow just outside the HQ block.

"Penny, what the hell!" She jerked her arm away and gave a furtive look around, especially at the wall of windows overlooking us. "Are you mad?"

"Why are you running away from me?" I demanded.

"Stop it," she hissed. "Stop it now."

"But I want to talk to you."

"Not here. Go away."

"I need to see you. I—"

"NAAFI." She suddenly relented, or else was too flustered to carry on this conversation outdoors. "TV recreation room in ten minutes." She turned and flounced off.

It would mean missing lunch and facing some awkward questions, but I raced across the green to the NAAFI bar as fast as I reasonably could.

The TV recreation room was a neglected area above the bar. If there was a big football match or sporting event on, most punters preferred to watch on the TV screen in the main bar below.

I arrived first and loitered by the door, anxious for Nicola to appear. It was so quiet, you could hear a pin drop. The bar was closed and nothing else seemed to happen in this building during the day.

Nicola slid through the door, angry spots of colour on her cheeks. "This is insane. We'll get caught," she said.

I reached for her. "I miss you. It's been ages."

"It has not."

"Well, it feels like ages." I moved to kiss her, but she wedged her arms in between and held me at bay.

"Penny, you can't do that. Run up to me in the street

like that. Haven't you heard a word I or Debs have said?"

"But I needed to see you."

"You don't get to 'need' anything from me. All I am is the itch you can't scratch. That's what your 'need' is. And if you want to be a lesbian in the army, you have to rein it in and play the same game we're all playing."

"I know, I know. I understand, and I promise I'll be more careful."

She relented, and I snuggled her in close for a long desperate kiss, wishing for more but knowing she was right. We had to choose our moments and this was one of the better ones.

"You know I can't get enough of you," I murmured into her ear.

She sighed in return, then murmured back, "I think I know what it is you can't get enough of."

There was a tinge of sadness to her tone that I chose to ignore. Instead, I kissed her again with all the intensity of emotion I had for her. I wanted her to know what she did to me. Maybe because there was no time or opportunity for sex. Maybe because this was simply a warm and loving embrace. The comfort of it stayed with me for the rest of the day and beyond, bolstering me through the dreary repetitiveness of training with the promise that I had a special someone waiting for me.

"I've told the rest, 1800 at the hockey pitch," Carol said the minute I turned up late for lunch. I looked at her in wonder. What was she talking about? I was still high on kissing Nicola. The real world had yet to encroach.

"For the extra drill training." She frowned. "Penny, we talked about this."

"Yeah." I shook myself. The real world always won. "I forgot for a moment."

She gave me a disbelieving look, but carried on. "So, what are your magic plans?"

Magic plans? I'd no idea. I figured I'd better find one fast.

At 1800, I was at the hockey pitch and raring to go.

"Okay, you lot." I addressed 3Plat, who had turned out in entirety in their gym tracksuits for a hard night's drill, bless their little regulation cotton socks.

"The best drill team out there is 4Plat, 'cause Evans sings to them in their sleep every night. But drill is all 4Plat have got. They're useless everywhere else, and I know we can beat 'em. Two Plat are a shower of smug bastards who think they have it all wrapped up, and 1Plat are jellyfish on stilts." Once again, I enjoyed finding my voice and giving everyone an earful. I was a natural leader *and* lover! I felt fantastic.

"The trick is music!" I announced my super magic plan. "And we're going to sing. Think about it. In every parade, they all march along to bands and drums and stuff. Music is the key, and that sneaky taff, Evans, knows it."

There was a ripple of excitement through my platoon. They were on board, ready for any challenge, and this one sounded like fun.

"Squad, atten'shun!" I yelled. They all snapped into file and came to attention sharpish. It was a joy to behold. "To the left, to the sound of 'I Beg Your Pardon (I Never Promised You a Rose Garden),' quick march!"

Off we went, around and around the hockey pitch, singing our hearts out. Lyn Anderson would have been proud. With each circuit, the duff ones improved their confidence, and the rest of us bolstered them along with song and camaraderie. We'd cracked it—all we needed was more time. It turned out to be such a fun thing to do that we agreed to practise at 1800 hours every Wednesday and Friday night from here on until the drill competition.

On the way back to our block, we bumped into Sgt Manners.

"Where have you lot been?" she barked.

We froze into one big google-eyed lump on the pavement. "Running, Sarge." I blurted the first thing that came to mind. We were all in our tracksuits, after all, so it seemed logical.

"What? All of you?"

"Yes, Sarge, they're helping me with my training." I was pushing it, but what else could we say?

"They need to be working on their own training. Like drill. You're all rubbish at drill."

There was no winning with Manners. If we'd told the truth, there'd still be something wrong in her eyes.

"Sorry, Sarge," we all mumbled.

"I suppose I'll just have to make do with two cups," she reasoned, then puffed out loud. "Pity, that." There was a moment of pointed silence before we caught the drift.

"Sorry, Sarge," we all said again.

Darkness fell. This was the evening we'd decided to "haunt" the new 2Coy before they got too firmly planted. I found our block filling up with girls from 1Plat and 2Plat.

"You can't all be in here," I said. "It'll look too obvious." God, but they could be such dunces. Everyone wanted a seat with a view and extra popcorn, and it wouldn't work like that. Even I, who'd been the master-mind behind it all, had to make sacrifices. My job was to find Judy and be a distraction while it all went down.

When Carol and Mo first levelled this idea at me, I was mulish. I didn't want to miss the fun. Then it dawned on me that having Hacker as an alibi might be the safest thing for me. I began to warm to the idea. Judy already hated my guts, but with me right beside her when it happened—how could she possibly blame me?

"Where shall we go?" The denser elements of 1Plat and 2Plat asked.

"Anywhere but here." I shooed them off. "Only the people involved need to be here. Bugger off."

They scooted off, leaving behind the ghost engineers and their lookouts. I ran over the plan one last time, though I trusted this lot.

"Mo, you and Joan keep the pole steady while Doreen and Elaine run the 'ghost' up it on the wire." It looked nothing like a ghost, but in the dark, tapping on a sec-ond-storey window it would have an alarming effect. "Brenda, Ruth, and Mandy are lookouts. Brenda takes the northeast corner of Block A. Ruth takes the south corner of Block B, overlooking the main green. Mandy..."

Mandy was skipping from toe to toe, overexcited and looking a little ludicrous. I could see the unhappy sideways glances the others gave her. No one trusted Mandy. I considered having her stay behind with Carol, who was keeping watch from our window, acting as the crow's nest lookout, but I feared Mandy wouldn't be content with that. She'd have to somehow be in the thick of it. I made an immediate command decision.

"Mandy, you come with me." Her face fell, so I sweetened the deal. "In case I need backup. After all, it is Judy." Mandy immediately brightened. This job had more kudos than keeping lookout around a corner. She agreed.

"Right, then. You all know what you're doing. Synchronize watches." We fumbled with our watches. "Okay. I'm off to find Judy," I said, implementing—to my mind—the most dangerous part of the plan. "Good luck, everyone, and don't be too long or you'll get caught." I tapped my watch face to impress the timeline on them.

"Good luck to *you!*" Joan gave me a knowing wink, her gaze straying to Mandy, who was chomping at the bit by the door. In answer, I stuck my tongue out at her. I was truly a hero in every sense.

Mandy and I nipped across the top floor to Hacker's private room. My hand trembled as I knocked, but I had to do it for the team. She didn't answer her door. Adams popped her head out of her own room across the way. "What do you want?"

The radio in her room was quietly playing The Partridge Family's "I Think I Love You," and it filtered out into the hallway.

"I was hoping for a word with Corporal Hacker."

"She's gone out for the night." Adams turned back to her room.

Shit. It had never occurred to me Judy might not be around. Who knew she had a private life? I'd always assumed she crept into a coffin on her downtime.

"Corporal?" Panic made me squeak. "Can I have a chat with you instead?"

"What can I do for you?" Adams, the kindly one as always, gave us her earnest attention. I felt almost guilty using her this way, but part of me was beginning to feel relieved Judy was out of the way. Adams was a much easier target and just as good an alibi.

"Well, you know I'm sitting the PT board soon?" I began, mirroring her wide-eyed earnestness.

"Yes."

"I wondered if you could tell me what to expect."

"I haven't a clue, Taylor. Surely you should be asking Corporal Bury?" She looked surprised, and I worried I'd fluffed it with my daft question.

"Okay, Corporal." My mind went blank. Just like that, all the questions I'd prepared for Judy had gone poof.

"Do you enjoy being in the army, Corporal?" Mandy's innocent question came to the rescue, most unexpectedly.

"Yes." Adams frowned.

"What made you join?" I chirped in, following Mandy's bizarre lead.

"Why are you asking all these questions?" Adams was clearly suspicious. "Aren't you happy?"

"Of course we are."

"We're interested, is all," Mandy added.

"Well, it's none of your business why I joined up. Now, if you'll excuse me, I have things to do." Adams turned away.

"Thank you," I blustered.

"What for?"

"For showing interest in us."

Adams frowned. "I don't know what you mean, Taylor."

Neither did I and it was becoming apparent. This was going badly.

"Thank you for being such a good training NCO." Mandy smiled sweetly. Was she actually being sincere? I was in a surreal world, caught between my own woeful under-preparedness, and Mandy being the one to save the day.

Adams blushed. "Thank you, Private Turner."

"We all think you're the best." I decided I might as

well join in. "Oh, and you won't tell Corporal Hacker what we've said." I pretended anxiety.

"Of course not." Adams blushed even deeper.

The small talk was over, but we'd managed to keep it going for about five minutes, all through "I Think I Love You" and well into Freda Payne's "Band of Gold."

On the way back to room two, we bumped into Doreen and Brenda running up the stairs, laughing hysterically.

"Shush. Adams might hear you," I scolded.

"Oh, Penny, you should have been there," Brenda said, around her uncontrollable giggling. "It was hilarious."

Doreen was just as bad, bent over double with laughter, and I felt jealous. My job had been so crucial but so boring and far away from the action.

"Rub it in, why don't you," I said. "Now let's get our ghost dismantled before anyone comes to check on us."

Joan and Mo were already in the room, dragging our ghost apart. It took minutes, and the ghost was no more than four coat hangers and a jacket from the wardrobe, and a mop and broom from the washroom. No one could ever have guessed at these objects' former lives. All that was left to do was to kick back and wait breathlessly for tomorrow's gossip to commence. We'd be lauded as geniuses.

It began to go wrong very quickly. From our window, we could see some senior ranks turning up at 2Coy's block. Then the phones started ringing in the NCO offices on the floor below, and despite the late hour, we could hear Adams pounding down the stairs to answer them.

We dispersed and pretended to be busy, unsure what to expect next. What none of us had foreseen was LCpl Adams dashing down the corridor, opening doors and calling everyone out into the corridor. I was in the ironing room and popped my head out to a sea of anxious faces.

"Go straight to your rooms and stand by your beds," Adams ordered. She looked worried and I began to feel uneasy. I gathered up my ironing and went to room two.

Mandy was looking out the window at the 2Coy block. "Some of them are getting their suitcases down from the top of their wardrobes," she said, in a mixture of disbelief and awe.

"There's a lot of them packing." Joan peeped over her shoulder. "Fuck. It wasn't that scary, was it?"

"Get away from that window, you silly buggers." I stormed over and yanked the curtains shut. "Didn't you hear Adams? She told us to stand by our beds, and that's what we're going to do. Act normal, for God's sake!" I was shaken. I had no idea what was going on across the way, but it didn't look good.

Adams came by, marked our names off a clipboard, and left without a word. She repeated this action throughout the entire building in every room. Everyone's nerves were screaming by the time we were sent to bed early. I suspect that was the point.

I didn't sleep well that night. My rendezvous with Nicola was shot to pieces, and I could only hope when she heard the news the next morning, she'd understand.

In my dreams, the accommodation block was on fire, but no one would believe me. I could smell the smoke but not see the flames.

"I wonder what's happened?" Joan's murmured question woke me the next morning. She was up early and moving about the room, quietly talking to Mandy, who was also awake and dressing.

"I don't know, but 2Coy's lights were on till the early hours of this morning," Mandy answered.

"How do you know?" I asked, swinging my legs out of bed. I stood up and stretched, glad to shake my unpleasant dream out of my system.

"I sat at the window watching. The officers left around 2330."

We woke Carol and, like us, the ghost caper and its fallout was the first thing on her mind. "We'll have to look surprised if we're told about it," she said.

"If we're even told about it." The thought occurred to me that we might get lucky and not be associated with last night's pandemonium.

No such luck. We were summoned to Manners's office after NAAFI morning break.

"This is it!" Mandy was giddy with fear and excitement.

We were told to sit on the floor, and on Manners's entrance, we scrambled to stand.

"Don't bother," she snapped, setting the tone. This was indeed an extraordinary meeting. She took her place at her desk and stared at us for ages, saying nothing. It was extremely unnerving, and in the overfull, stuffy room, the temperature, as well as the level of anxiety, rocketed.

Finally, Manners broke the stony silence. "Somebody— and I believe that person or persons is in this room— played a really stupid practical joke last night." Some idiot chuckled at the back. I could have thumped her.

"So, some of you know already? Some of you think that's funny, do you?" Manners's tone was eerily calm. The chuckling stopped instantly. She fixed her gaze steadily on Mandy and me.

I wasn't the one chuckling! Panic began to eat the heart out of me.

"And when I find out who was involved, they'll wish they were never born," she continued, unblinking. I was unnerved. Beside me, waves of panic washed off Mandy. God only knew what her face looked like. Mandy hadn't a poker face. She was more of a tabloid—big print and questionable content.

There was another long period of silence. This time everyone in the room was sober with anxiety. It was like waiting for a guillotine to fall. I didn't dare take my eyes off Manners, and tried to look as innocent as possible. Eventually, her stony glare broke away from me, and she barked, "Get out of my office. Now!"

We scrambled to our feet, and as I was going through the door, Manners bellowed, "Taylor, Turner. I want a word with you two."

My stomach hit my shoes. I was shaking and dared not meet Mandy's eyes, though I could feel her looking at me in stunned silence. We stood side by side at attention before the desk.

"I don't care what you have to say. I wouldn't believe a word of it anyway." Manners came around the desk. My eyes followed her until she was in front of me, breathing heavily up into my face. "Taylor, I know you were behind what happened last night."

"But, Sarge—"

"Shut it! Lance Corporal Adams has already told me how you were conveniently talking to her last night when the *incident* occurred. Good little alibi, that, except I *know* it was you. I can feel it in my water like a kidney stone."

She moved away from me to face Mandy—the weakest link as far as I was concerned, and Manners knew it, too.

"Fifteen—yes, fifteen—trainees are leaving today and all because of you, Turner."

Mandy jumped. Her whole body must have lifted an inch off the floor. From out of the side of my eye, I could see her trembling all over.

"Don't, not even for one minute, be stupid enough to think you've got away with this. I'll be watching you two *intently* from here on in, and if you so much as fart in the wrong direction, you'll be out of this army quicker than your feet can touch the ground. Understand?"

I was shaking so much, I couldn't speak.

"I said, do you understand?"

"Yes, Sergeant," Mandy and I blurted in unison.

"Get out!"

We nearly fell out the door, gasping in the corridor like landed fish.

"Look at my hands." Mandy held them out. They shook as badly as my own.

We moved as fast as our quivering knees would carry us along the corridor and away from Manners's office, in case she decided to call us back and have another go.

Around the corner, we bumped into LCpl Adams heading the way we had come. She took one look at us and suppressed a knowing smirk, making me wonder if she'd had the rough edge of Manners's tongue today, too.

"Look at you two," she said. "You're as white as ghosts."

Chapter 11

It was week five and the day of the PTI board came around almost too quickly. I was as prepared as well as I'd ever be, and part of me wanted it over with. Either I was going to be a physical training instructor in the military, or I'd become a civilian again. I knew there was no way I could sit behind a desk for the rest of my army career.

I was one of the first to turn up at the gym and took my time getting ready. There was little conversation since we were all nervous.

Cpl Bury came to the locker room and gave us a pep talk before we started. "There are three officers on the board. I don't need to remind you to be polite at all times. You will be asked to do warm-ups, play games, give instructions, and participate in a gym class. You will not be asked to do anything we haven't practised, okay? It's going to be a gruelling afternoon, but I know you're all fit for it. Good luck."

On her command, we lined up and marched into the gym, past the table where the board sat, and continued around the gym until called to a halt.

"About face!" Bury ordered. We spread out facing the board and began our first warm-up exercise. The warm-up lasted half an hour, and I was a sweaty mess by the end of it.

"Taylor," Bury shouted, "Are you all right?"

"Yes, Corporal," I snapped back. I was furious that she drew attention to me. I was no more exhausted than anyone else.

Bury gave us all a glare. "Anyone not coping should dismiss themselves. The board will understand."

Why single me out like this? I was coping as well as anyone else. I was furious with Cpl Bury. There was a smirk on Sonya Kent's face, and I was determined to wipe it off.

This was by no means a two-horse race. Several other girls were red hot within their own specialties, but I was a strong all-rounder and so was Sonya. Plus, this was her second time around, so she had a massive advantage over all of us. I resented her smug attitude, as if she had it already sewn up. Despite Cpl Bury's seeming lack of confidence in me, I'd show her and Sonya Kent a thing or two.

I got my chance soon enough, when we were ordered to collect the hockey gear from storage and form two teams. I made sure I was on the opposite team from Sonya. I'd been invited to try out for the England team in 1966, so I was no slouch. The game quickly developed into a battle between Sonya and me, with me getting the better of her. The difference was, I involved my team, where she tried to do it all herself and dragged her side down with her, much to their frustration. I was surprised she exposed her lack of delegation and team spirit so openly. To me, that was a huge failing, and I hoped the board saw it the same way I did.

I felt good afterward, both physically and mentally. The whistle blew, and we tidied the kit away and moved on to netball, another of my favourite sports.

The games section went on for over three hours. The time passed quickly for me, but for some, it was too much. One by one, several girls faded away to sit on the sidelines and shout encouragement during the volleyball match, the last of our team games.

The final exercise was commands. We took it in turns to come forward and project the given commands in a clear, firm voice. Fortunately, because the army did everything in alphabetical order, I was one of the last to go and by then, I'd got my breath back and performed well.

Cpl Bury marched us back to the locker room, where we changed back into uniform and waited as, one by one, again in alphabetical order, we were presented before the board to hear their critique and assessment. Each individual then had to directly exit the sports block, so we didn't hear how we'd all done. It was very tense as the crowd dwindled down to me, the last in line on this course.

Cpl Bury waited in the locker room with us, organising who went in, and when. As we thinned out, she became relaxed and chatty, until there was just the two of us remaining.

"You were pretty good out there, Taylor," she said. "Seriously, I was impressed."

"Do you know the results, Corporal?"

She shook her head. "No. Only the board knows."

"Private Taylor!" The call came from the hall. I puffed my cheeks and straightened my beret.

"Good luck." Bury slapped me on the shoulder as I marched past her and into the gym.

"Stand at ease." Major Travis introduced herself as the commander of the Army School of Physical Training. She checked and rechecked the paperwork before her, while I stood at ease with a thumping heart. Had I been good enough?

"Frankly, I'm surprised you made it through, Taylor. You looked like you'd keel over after the warm-up session," Major Travis said, not looking up from her notes. I wasn't sure how to respond and again felt resentful that Cpl Bury had drawn attention to me. Was I going to pay for it now?

The major continued. "It says here that you missed training because of a stint in the MRS."

"Yes, ma'am. Suspected appendicitis, ma'am."

"Have you properly recovered?" She squinted at me over her wire-rimmed glasses.

"I have, ma'am." I began to wonder if Bury had drawn attention to me deliberately. Suddenly, I could see how my hospitalization could work as a bonus. Maybe Bury had done me a favour after all?

"Hmm. Although you started out poorly, you progressed as the session went on, showing stamina..." She began her assessment and I zoned out. There was a loud buzzing in my head. There was no bonus. I guessed from her officious tone that I'd flunked it. I'd lost too much ground with my fucking grumbling appendix. I could have kicked myself. There I'd been, shagging half the MRS, while my career ended up in the bed pan.

"Dismissed." Major Travis glared at me. I jumped. I'd drifted off and not listened to a word. I stood dazed for a spilt second. Long enough for Cpl Bury to poke me in the back.

"You can go now," she muttered.

"Thank you, ma'am." I saluted and marched out like a robot—a robot with wobbly legs.

Cpl Bury followed me out to the hall with the exit doors. "Well done," she said and proffered her hand. "Welcome to the ASPT."

Army School of Physical Training? "I made it?" I must have sounded like a fool.

"What did the Major just say, you nitwit?"

"I zoned out. I never heard a word," I admitted.

Bury threw her head back and roared with laughter. "I did exactly the same thing when I qualified."

I started laughing, too. "I qualified? I'm an AKI?" AKI was army abbreviation for an Assistant Instructor. It was hard to believe I'd made it. I'd wanted it so much.

"Yes, you're an AKI now." She had a huge, warm smile that I'd never noticed before. Probably because she reserved it for her own people, and I was one of those now—well, almost. "Call me Bones," she said. "All the PTIs do."

Now *that* was a real welcome.

"I'm an AKI. An Assistant Instructor," I repeated, just to make sure. It tasted delicious in my mouth. I couldn't wait to call my mum. I must have lost my marbles, because I grabbed Bury by the waist and lifted her off the ground and swung her around. She was friendly like that, the sort of girl you could relax and be yourself with, once all the army business was out of the way.

"Put me down, you big oaf!"

"I've done it! I've done it!"

Cpl Bury wriggled away. "Private Taylor," she said sharply, bringing me to my senses. "Get to the cookhouse and have your tea."

"Yes, Corporal." I felt awkward now. I'd embarrassed us both. Thank God no one else was around to witness my high spirits. I turned to go, momentarily flattened by my own enthusiasm.

"And, Taylor," Bury called after me.

"Yes, Corporal?"

"Be at the bar tonight. We'll be celebrating, okay?" Her wink was so sly I almost missed it. The skies turned blue again and my smile came back.

"You bet, Corporal."

I ran to the cookhouse, my kit bag bouncing at my hip. One Coy was there for their meal, and all eyes were on me as I barged in the swing doors. I raised my arms in the air, turned my back on them, bent over, and wiggled my bum.

"This better mean you passed," Mandy yelled.

"No, it means mutton for dinner," Joan said drily, but gave me a big grin.

"Yes, it bloody well does!" I yelled back. "I passed. I mean, not the mutton." There was a huge shout and suddenly I was being pummelled left, right, and centre by my mates. I was the first in our company to devise the first steps in their army career, and it felt great, as well as being a bolster for those coming after me.

One of the girls who had failed the PTI board came over. "You were brilliant, Penny. You deserved it." She told me Sonya had taken the other place.

I didn't give a rat's arse about Sonya Kent and her sideways looks anymore. I'd made it and that was all that mattered.

"Thank you. I'm sorry you didn't make it. What are you going to do now?" I asked.

"Plan B, I'm going to be a driver. I was a bit out of my league in there, so I'm kind of pleased."

"Good luck with the driving." I meant it. I was so happy, and I wanted the whole world to be happy along with me.

The good feeling continued into the afternoon. Payday!

As with everything in the army, this was strictly choreographed. We had to march down to pay office and line up outside. Each soldier was called individually and had to march into the office and salute the Pay Officer smartly. The pay officer was the unsmiling Captain Rodgers, who looked so miserable, we joked that it was her own money she was doling out.

"At ease," she droned. "Name, rank, number." She didn't bother to look up from her payroll. In all the time I spent at Guildford, I never once saw the colour of her eyes.

Rodgers pointed to where I should sign. Then she passed over my wages envelope, which I had to put in my left pocket, then salute, turnabout, and exit on the march.

Outside, I returned to my place and waited for over an hour as 3Plat got paid. My wages envelope burnt a hole in my left-hand pocket. Seven whole pounds, before deductions for food and accommodation, which left us with around six pounds for ourselves. Like everyone else, I was itching to head to the NAAFI later that evening and have a beer. The place would be packed with merry revellers.

I was on a high. First, I'd aced my PTI board, then payday—so it was only right to develop a headache.

I had to see Nicola. I could celebrate with my friends over a few pints at the NAAFI, but what I really wanted was to kiss Nicola. I wanted to share my victory and happiness with my lover, if only for a few minutes.

"With all the excitement, I think I've got a headache," I announced. I was at the canteen with Carol and Mandy and we'd just finished dinner. I had a few hours' free time and decided to saunter over from the cookhouse to MRS. Nicola was on duty.

"I'll come with you." Mandy stood, too. I sighed. She was such a limpet.

"Okay. Let's take this wounded soldier to find a caring medic," I agreed.

Clearly, Mandy was itching to tell me something, so I let her tag along. To be honest, there was no way I could dislodge her when she got in a clingy mood like this. Mandy was the perfect cover. I knew Nicola was too cautious to be totally pleased at my impromptu visit. Mandy in tow made it more authentic for spying eyes.

We trotted along to the MRS, "So, what's up?" I asked, since Mandy seemed to need a prompt—never a good sign.

"That bitch Judy put me on extra duty on Saturday night."

"What for?"

Judy was indeed a bitch, but usually she only meted out punishment where it was due.

"I left a mess in ablutions," Mandy mumbled, twin spots of angry colour on her cheeks relaying her guilt.

"That was sort of stupid."

Mandy was often sort of stupid. I gave thanks I hadn't been anywhere near her that day, or I'd have had a lousy Saturday night lined up, too.

"She's a cow and she's been out to get us from—"

"Hang on a minute, Mandy," I said, not liking this "us" language. "You left a mess, and she caught you—"

"Only because I hadn't time to clean—"

"Doesn't matter. You left a mess, even for a minute, and she caught you."

"I'm going to get her back, and I need your help."

"Oh, no. Keep me out of this," I protested. Hadn't Mandy learned her lesson by now? "We're the grunts, Mandy. We don't get even. We survive. Got that? Hasn't two nights cleaning the parade ground on your knees taught you anything?"

Mandy's face darkened at the memory. I'd inadvertently fuelled her bad mood. She was in such foul form over Judy, it was beginning to affect her training. I'd had my run-ins, too, but I was still able to shake it off and concentrate on what *I* wanted from the army—namely the place on the PTI course that I'd just bagged. Even thinking about it made me smile.

Mandy didn't have anything like that. As far as I could tell, she had no ambition and was thoughtless as to her career trajectory. I wasn't sure why she was even here. It was as if she'd drifted through the camp gates on a whim. She fell into a glum silence and trudged along beside me. After a second, I nudged her with my elbow. We'd arrived at the steps to the MRS entrance.

"Just get Saturday night over and done with, and I'll treat you to coffee at Redeemers on Sunday afternoon, okay?" Redeemers was the Christian coffee house on site. I wasn't particularly enthralled with the place, finding it gloomy and the coffee crap, but Mandy had taken to going there. She immediately brightened. It didn't take much to lift her little helium-filled heart.

We rang the bell and Nicola appeared from farther down the corridor. She came over to let us in and my heart missed a beat at every step that brought us closer together.

"What can I do for you two?" she snapped, even less pleased at seeing me than predicted.

"I've got a headache." I moaned, hamming it up. "Could I have an aspirin please, nurse?"

"Come in and I'll get you some." Her manner was still frosty toward me, but I thought there was a special little glint in her eye.

"She's just been selected for the PTI's course and she's overexcited!" Mandy felt the need to explain.

"Has she now?" Nicola said, and the special little glint flared brighter. "Go in there." She pointed to a treatment room. Mandy made to follow.

"Not you. She doesn't need you holding her hand." She closed the outer door in Mandy's face.

Once inside the treatment room, she cupped my face and kissed me. "Who's a clever girl, then?"

"I am." I tried to return the kiss, but she pushed me away and turned toward the medicine cabinet. "I didn't think I'd make it."

"*I* did," Nicola said proudly. "When you put your mind to something, you can..." She trailed off and the frostiness seeped back.

"I'm sorry about not coming over the other night. We were put in lockdown. Can I see you later?" I asked, perhaps a little too eagerly. Her back stiffened.

"I heard about the ghost prank. What a stupid thing to do. I hope you hadn't a part in it?"

"What? No way. Not me."

"That's the kind of behaviour puts you in the spotlight, and believe me, we gays do not need any extra attention." She glared, clearly struggling to believe me.

Okay, so I was lying, but I somehow sensed that even if I wasn't, I was going to get this lecture anyway. As a person, Nicola was suspicious to the marrow. I was beginning to wonder if she was paranoid, too. For all her talk of SIB, I hadn't seen a sign of them and I was in my fifth week here.

"So?" I got the conversation back on track. "Can I see you?"

"I'm on nights again." She grabbed a packet from the cabinet. "Here, take two of these now and again in four hours." She gave me a strip of pills and filled a paper cup with water.

"Maybe I can drop by?" I swallowed the pills.

"No."

"Please, just for a short while."

"I said yes last time and look where it got me—stood up because of some childish codology. I'm not sitting around here waiting to see if you can make it or not."

"That was hardly my fault."

Were we having an argument? We were, we were having our first argument and it felt... Ugh! I tried a different tack. "Aw, come on. I'll be leaving in two weeks, and I'd like to spend some more time with you before I go."

I walked up behind her, placed my hands on her hips and turned her round. She was near to tears.

"Please?" I pleaded.

She allowed me to kiss her, though I felt an inner resistance I didn't understand. She wanted this as much as me, didn't she? Surely, she felt the same way.

"Come back after eight. It gets quieter then," she said. But she looked far from happy.

The NAAFI bar was packed. Payday had ensured that. I found my gang in the far corner. I squeezed in with much back-slapping and congratulations from anyone who hadn't seen me yet. I was floating in a bubble of wellbeing until Mandy popped it. She felt compelled to finish the conversation she'd started on the way over to the MRS. If I hadn't a headache then, she'd given me one now.

She leaned over and whispered in my ear. "Penny, I've thought of a way to get Hacker."

I pulled away and ignored her, happy to be distracted by the offer of a congratulatory pint from Carol. When she moved off to the bar, though, Mandy was in my face again.

"But I need your help." She looked furtively left and right. The rest of our table was in high spirits and no one paid any attention to us. "I'm going to put wet tea leaves in her forage cap," she said, proud of the idea.

My head snapped around. She had my full attention now. "Are you mad? I hope you've a job lined up on civvy street."

"No, listen. It's brilliant. I put the tea dregs in her cap, and she doesn't know until she wears it. How can she know it was us? Isn't it hysterical?"

"Us? Oh, no, Mandy. Keep me well out of this one." I was adamant, and my voice became hard-edged. "Things are going good for me, and I'm not letting you cock it up." Then a thought occurred. "Her forage cap is part of her No2s. She wears it on duty. You're not seriously going to douse her in wet tea leaves before going on duty?" No2s were worn for NCO duty or else going on parade. I was agog at Mandy's stupidity.

She broke out laughing. "I know," she said. "It's brilliant, isn't it?"

"No, it's not. It's fucking moronic, and I want nothing to do with it. Is that clear?" Carol came back with my beer, and I turned away and hurled myself into other, saner conversations.

An hour in, I decided it was time to scuttle over and visit Nicola.

"That corporal is waving at you," Mandy said. "Isn't

she one of them PTIs?"

Corporal Bury signalled me to join her from the door. This might be as good a time as any to say goodbye to my mates and swing by the MRS, once I found out what Bones wanted.

"Don't wait up for me." I squeezed out from my table and joined Bones at the door.

"A few of us are upstairs." She thumbed the stairway leading to the recreation rooms on the next floor.

I never bothered with these rooms, preferring the main bar, though some people went upstairs on busy nights where there was more seating.

I followed Bones to an upstairs room where the partition between NCOs and privates had been opened. There were only six PTIs and most faces I recognised, except for one. My attention was immediately drawn to a pretty, blonde girl with a cheeky grin. This girl was new. I hadn't met her before. As I approached, she slyly appraised me from top to toe and seemed to like what she saw.

"We want to buy you a drink, Penny. Now that you're one of us," Bones said. "What will it be?"

"A snakebite, please." I sat beside the newcomer and was introduced.

"Penny, this is Dotty Bloom. She came over from

Aldershot yesterday. Sara is posted to Germany and Dotty is replacing her."

"Hello," I said shyly.

"Hi, and I hear congratulations are in order."

We shook hands and butterflies swarmed in the pit of my belly. Her grin got even more wicked. Dotty would be a right handful, but I wanted to grab her anyway.

"So, what did you do in Aldershot?" I was grasping at straws to keep her talking to me, though the minute I said it out loud, it sounded stupid.

"I'm a PTI." She looked at me puzzled. Why else would she be sitting here with this lot?

"You're up next, Dotty." Sara called over from the dart board.

"Is that your real name?" My next question was even stupider.

Dotty stood. "It's a nickname. I'll tell you about it sometime." She gave me a wink and walked away. I watched her backside sway like some sort of dimwit.

"Here."

I was pulled out of my trance when Bones set a pint of snakebite before me.

"Where's Sonya?" I noticed she was missing.

Bones shrugged, and it became clear that the rest of the PTIs found Sonya as engaging as I had. Interesting, considering this was her second time around and she still hadn't made any mates. It said a lot, since this was a friendly bunch and I suspected a lot of them were either family, or else unconcerned about the gay world.

"So, what happens next? Though I may have already been told and blocked it out, with the shock of it all." I diplomatically changed the conversation away from Sonya.

"That depends on when the next course starts," Bones told me. "They last three months. Sometimes, if you've to wait a long time for the next course to start, you can be lucky enough to join an existing one for a pre-course run. That's a good thing."

"When did the last course start?" I asked.

"Two weeks ago, so you're lucky. You'll have the advantage of the pre-course." She smiled. She really did wish me well.

I checked my watch. I'd be late for Nicola, and I daren't let her down, not after the last fiasco. "You'll have to excuse me," I said and swallowed the last of my drink. "I have another celebration going on downstairs and I've been away too long."

"Well, go then," Sara said casually. "We didn't expect you to stay all night."

"Thanks for the drink. See you guys later."

I was halfway to the exit when I heard a stampede of

feet behind me. They'd ambushed me! Six giggling PTIs dragged me off my feet. They bodily picked me up and gave me the bumps amid much drunken hysteria. I shrieked good-naturedly, accepting that this was part of their little welcome ritual, though all the while, I was very conscious of Dotty with her hand on my bottom, copping a feel.

"...seven, eight, nine, ten!" they chorused, then cheered as I was upended back onto my feet.

"That's for the whirly-gig you gave me this afternoon, Taylor." Bones laughed and raised her glass.

My head was spinning, and my balance was off for a few seconds. I shook with laughter.

Dotty took hold of my arm. "Sit down for a while," she said.

"I've really got to go." I put my hand over hers and gave it a little squeeze. "Bye...for now."

"**A**re we allowed to try every bed?"

"No, you numpty. I'll have to remake them all."

"Not as if you've got anything else to do." The place was empty. Guildford training camp must be the healthiest place in the United Kingdom.

I stroked Nicola's face gently. We were lying together

on a bed in one of the side wards. I cupped her chin and kissed her, her lips opened for me to explore. Everything about Nicola intoxicated me, from her kisses to her creamy skin to her musky scent of desire when I pulled down her regulation knickers and stockings.

I loved the way she could be so bossy, wanting control over everything, but could give it up so readily when it mattered for our love play, like she had at Sandy's house that weekend. She was the more experienced of the two of us, yet she allowed me to use her body as a learning ground. She let my confidence as a lover grow and was gifted in teaching me new things. Things I could never have imagined in a thousand years and was eager to build on. I also loved time like this with her, when intimacy was everything. I lay there exploring her mouth with my tongue, fascinated by the sensation a kiss could evoke in me. Then, suddenly, Nicola had me flat on my back and was tugging at my tracksuit. I liked this side of Nicola, too. She was a tigress if I pressed the right button. Trouble was, I never knew exactly where that button was.

She stripped my top off effortlessly with an expertise only medics used to dealing with front-line battle wounds had. I suppose I was lucky there were no scissors handy, or I'd be slinking home in tatters.

"God, but I love your tits." She fell upon them like

they were manna from heaven. I let her devour me while I fumbled less expertly with the buttons and zippers of her uniform. I managed to undress her down to the waist and revealed a hot pink lace bra—definitely not regulation. I eased her breast out and began to gorge.

"My turn now," I growled. She loved it when I growled. So much so, she stuck two fingers deep into me. I heard bells ring and I growled even louder.

"Who the fuck is that?" She'd just found the spot, but quickly whipped her fingers away. She lifted off me, leaving me chilled and unfocused. The bell rang again. The night bell by the back entrance.

"Christ, Christ, fuck, fuck!" Nicola was pulling the top of her uniform back into place. Her panic was contagious. I started scrabbling around the floor for my trackie bottoms and top, my bum unceremoniously in the air. It would have been comical if we hadn't both been frigid with fright.

Someone rapped hard on the window nearest us. "Anyone in there? Hello?"

Nicola squeaked and ran to twitch the curtain open a fraction. I flopped flat on my belly and contemplated crawling under the bed.

"Yes. What is it?" Nicola cleared her throat and tried to sound officious.

"I've been ringing and ringing the bell. Where were you?" A clipped voice came back. Damn, an NCO. No one else would talk to a nurse like that. A miffed NCO, too, from the sound of it.

"I'll be with you directly, ma'am." Nicola confirmed it was an officer and swished the curtain back in place. "Get out of here," she hissed at me.

"How?" I was nearly hysterical.

"Out the window. Forget the rest of your clothes. I'll get them to you later." Nicola as good as ran out of the room to the back door, from where I heard another barrage of ringing.

That was all right for her to say. My knickers had my nametag on them! I cautiously flicked the corner of the curtain, half-expecting the nameless officer to be waiting outside to grab me. All was clear. Down the hall, I could hear Nicola open the outer door, then voices. There was more than one visitor. I skivvied about under the bed one more time for my bra and knickers, shoved them up my tracksuit top, and opened the window as quietly as I could.

I leapt out that window like a commando. Well, I *was* commando. It was an excellent leap, and I sailed over the flowerbeds like a terrified gazelle on the Serengeti. Then I legged it for seven hundred yards before ducking behind a hedge near the main car park and shoving my underwear into my voluminous pockets. I took several deep, cooling inhalations before emerging and sauntering casually toward my block. My chest was still hurting from the hammering my heart had given it.

Christ, that was close. Part of me was elated, part was terrified, and after walking a bit, I found I'd gone a full circle and was back at the MRS. It had been half an hour since my impromptu exit, and all looked quiet. I hovered by the back door, frightened to ring, in case Nicola had patients or NCOs to deal with. Even as I considered slinking off again, she appeared from farther up the corridor. She saw me, and her hand flew to her chest and she paled.

Her step quickened to open the door. "What do you want?" she hissed.

"I was worried about you," I whispered. "Who was it? Are they in there now?"

"It was Corporal Pike. One of her recruits had a nosebleed that wouldn't stop. They've gone."

"Then, why are we whispering?" I moved to enter but she held a hand out and stopped me.

"No, Penny."

I halted on the top step, confused.

"Tonight was madness and far too close for comfort," she said. "Look, you're leaving in two weeks. It's crazy to sneak around camp like this. We're jeopardizing our careers. I don't want to be the next Helen and Sandy."

"Who said we'd be—"

"I'm sorry, Penny." Her eyes suddenly filled with tears. "I'm finishing with you. We're through. I can't keep running risks like this. Debs is right. It's going to ruin my career. You, you're just starting out on so many levels. You're clueless and careless, and I don't want any part of it."

"Well, fine by me!" I backed down the steps, my cheeks and anger flaming. "I can't keep up with your bloody moods anyway."

"That's not fair. You have no idea what living like this does to you."

But I'd already turned my back and was stomping away. I'd just been dumped. This was meant to be the greatest week of my life. I'd got my AKI against all the odds. I wanted to be with Nicola, my lover. I wanted fun and sex and...well, sex. I *liked* sex and I damned well wasn't going to apologise for it. Nicola had her chance and threw me away. She'd only had to wait two weeks and I'd have been gone anyway. Unbelievable. Well, to hell with her. This was the army, and there were plenty more fish to fry.

Chapter 12

Our secret drill practices were going well.

"I really think we've cracked it," Carol said, after a particularly successful evening stomping all over the hockey pitch with Lyn Anderson rattling around in our brains.

It was late, and we were in our room, lounging around and getting ready for bed, feeling tired and relaxed after our exercise, and partly elated at how good it had gone.

"We're seriously in with a chance at the cup. You should be a staff sergeant, Penny. You've got the lungs for it," she added.

"Yeah, you could frighten 1Plat into dropping their knickers faster than Meeke." Joan poked me in the side.

"No. Me! Me! I'm Meeke!" Mandy, contrary to the rest of us, was in a hyper mood and leapt to her feet, stomping up and down, knees high and arms swinging in a clownish march.

"Corporal Meeke smacks yer bum cheek. Two, three," she sang out in marching time. We laughed at her mimicking of Meeke, whom Mandy was certain was "one of them," and that, of course, made her even giddier.

"To the loo, two, three." She marched to the door and snatched it open. "If you want to have a pee follow me, two, three." She stomped off into the corridor.

We followed, highly amused. Mandy was a nut, but good entertainment when she wasn't being moody.

"Knickers down. Stand easy, Meeke will have a nice wee squeezy, two, three." The other room doors opened and the rest of the platoon emerged and began to laugh at her antics.

"Squad halt, left incline, drop your knickers anytime!" She marched along the corridor, past all the opened doors toward ablutions. "Knickers down, bend over, let Corporal Mee—" The door to ablutions banged open as if a tornado had blown off its hinges.

Cpl Hacker stood there with a soap bag and a face like thunder. I've never seen a crowd disperse so fast. Girls were jamming each other in their doorways to get offside as quickly as possible. Joan and I nearly did the same thing, except I gave an extra hip wiggle that got me through and under my bed covers in seconds flat. All of us bounded into bed like naughty toddlers, pulled the bedclothes up to our ears, and pretended to sleep. It didn't matter that Judy had seen us in the corridor mere seconds ago. With a bit of luck, by the time she'd finished skinning Mandy's carcass, she'd have forgotten about us, or be sated enough by the taste of human flesh not to care. My hopes were on the latter. Judy forgot nothing, but like some ancient god, could be appeased with human sacrifice. I was absolutely terrified I'd be somehow dragged into this.

Our door flew open, and we all drew in our breath. We were dead. Simple as that.

Mandy came in—walking like Frankenstein, her arms stretched out before her and her eyes wide open, on stalks. It was so unexpected and unnerving, I forgot to feign sleep. Mandy threw back her bedclothes and slid under them before closing her eyes just as Judy flew in after her.

"*You!*" Judy leaned over the bed and waved a finger in Mandy's face. "You are *not* sleepwalking! I know your game, Turner." Mandy's eyes sprung open, but she had the sense to keep her mouth shut.

"My office, tomorrow morning, 0800 sharp. You will regret this, Turner! It will give me the greatest pleasure to make sure you do." With that, she thundered out and slammed the door behind her. We were quiet as the tomb for the next few minutes until her footsteps disappeared and the swing doors clattered closed behind her, telling us she was off our wing.

Mandy sat up. "I thought I was going to pee myself, I was so frightened." Her hand went to her chest. She was white as the sheet around her waist. "That woman is mad."

"You really did set yourself up for it." I peeled back my bedclothes and got up to undress, put on my pyjamas, and got back into bed, though it was barely dark outside. That's how weird the evening had been. Joan and Carol followed suit. We were all shaken and subdued. The only good thing out of the whole brouhaha was that, for once, I hadn't been caught up in Mandy's backwash.

"She's going to ruin my Saturday night again," Mandy snivelled. "It's not fair. You all made me do it."

"Oh, no you don't," Carol scolded. "That nonsense was all your own doing, and you know it. You just had to show off for the whole floor."

Mandy sniffed derisively, but let it go. "Penny," she turned to me. "I'm definitely going to do it now."

"Do what?" I asked sleepily. My head was, for once, snuggled into my lumpy pillow just right, and I was weary. Extreme terror can do that to a body—drain every last ounce of strength out of it.

"The tea leaves idea."

"Mandy," I said, wriggling under the bedcovers cosily. "You're as thick as a bar of army soap. You'll never learn."

Actually, Mandy did learn something about army soap. She had to wash down ablutions singlehandedly the next Saturday night while we were all out at the NAAFI bar, raising a pint to her—our comrade missing in action.

I was kidding myself to think that I could get over Nicola easily. I missed her. I hadn't seen her since that last eventful Friday. On this day, I knew she changed shift, and looked out for her at breakfast. Lots of other medics were there, but not her, so I concluded she must be on the early shift.

"I've got a headache," I announced. I had to go see her.

"Another one?" Carol was surprised.

"I'm getting them a lot lately," I said. "Too much military law cramming." I left the table quickly to avoid any more questions. "I'm going to get some tablets."

Once I got to the MRS, I was unsure what to do, so I went around the back and loitered, trying to garner some courage and come up with a decision. Stay or go.

"What do you want?" Sgt Jones, an NCO at the MRS, came up behind me, obviously on her way to work. I was so used to sneaking in and out the back door, I'd forgotten it was the medics' work entrance.

"Good morning, Sergeant. I've got a headache and wondered if I could have some tablets, please?"

"So why are you hanging out around here? You need to be around the front."

"I was just heading that way."

Jones was the kind of person who had no time for anything or anyone. If your leg was hanging off, she'd tell you to hop it.

"Might as well come on in this door now." She ploughed past me without so much as a sideways glance. I followed her into the waiting area, where she signalled I take a seat with that morning's other losers.

"But I just want a painkiller," I whined. Now that I was in the actual MRS and could hear voices from rooms farther up the corridor, I felt really ill. The place was emotionally claustrophobic—the lighting too bright, the smells all horrible and wrong.

"Are you all right?" Sgt Jones asked. "You've gone white." The girl beside me began to take an intense interest in my plight and I wanted to tell her to piss off. This was not the time for Jones to pay me any attention. A sheen of sweat broke out on my forehead. I could hear Nicola's voice and suddenly wanted to vomit with nerves.

"Platoon and NCO?" Jones snapped. "I think the MO should have a look at you."

"I only want a painkill—"

Her glare stopped me cold.

"Three Plat, Corporal Hacker," I answered, and she wandered off to call Judy.

Cherie came out of the nearest treatment room and called, "Private Singleton." The nosy girl next to me stood. "Come in here and I'll change that dressing."

Cherie didn't acknowledge me at all. Not that I cared, but what if Nicola treated me like that? I didn't think I could stand it. *I'll cry if she does.*

"Private Taylor?" I looked up to find Debs Doherty beckoning me. "The doctor will see you now."

I followed her into the MO's surgery, which somehow felt marginally safer than the regular treatment rooms, probably because Nicola and I had never made love in this room. *Made love.* My heart lurched.

Debs dumped me with Fraser and left. Happy old sop that he was, he smiled up at me from his desk. "Hello again, young lady. You don't look too tucker. What can I do for you?"

"I've had a headache since 0700, sir. I only need a tablet."

"I'm the doctor, young lady, and I'll decide what you need. Now let's have a look at you." He patted me on the head. "How's the tummy? No more pains? I want to be certain there's nothing else wrong. An appendix can be a sneaky thing." He opened his bag. "Bother, I've left my stethoscope in the car." He snapped his bag shut. "Nurse, take her vitals. I'll be back in a moment."

"Yes, sir." Nicola's voice came from behind me. I stiffened and kept my back to her.

"Back in a jiffy." He left us alone.

"Can you remove your jacket, please, and roll up your sleeve." Her tone was coolly professional.

Tears jabbed my eyes. I removed my jacket, deliberately keeping my back to her until I got myself under control.

"Sit down, please."

I sat, but didn't dare look at her as I laid out my bare arm. Nothing happened. Time seemed to stand still, until I wondered if she was still in the room. I eventually looked up and found her standing across from me, gazing distractedly out the window.

"You look tired," I said. I was being kind, she looked absolutely haggard.

"I'm not sleeping very well."

"Neither am I." I rose to move toward her. "I need to

see you. I've missed you so much."

She glanced over at me and I melted.

"Sit." She pushed me back to the chair, wrapped a blood pressure armband around my arm, and then put a thermometer in my mouth.

There was silence for another minute or two, and I spent the time straining to hear if Fraser was on his way back. I so wanted to talk to her alone. After a minute, she took the thermometer away and removed the armband.

"Your blood pressure's up a little, but your temperature's okay," she said mechanically.

"I need to see you." I reached for her.

She twisted away. "I've made a decision and I'm sticking to it."

"But why, when it's killing us and we've so little time?" I pleaded. "I miss you. Don't you miss me?"

She turned her back to me and put away the equipment. "Of course I miss you."

"Then, we should see each other again. It's stupid not to."

"No. No, it's not," she snapped. "I've got to get you out of my system." Her voice went soft. "I love you, Penny, and I know you don't love me. So, I have to stick to my decision."

My heart skipped a beat, but before I could reply, Dr Fraser breezed in. "Well, how is she, nurse?"

"She's as fit as a fiddle, sir."

I tried to catch her gaze, but she avoided me. She wasn't going to risk me being admitted again. Nicola left the surgery, and Dr Fraser continued my medical, checking my heart and lungs.

"You seem fine. I'll give you a strong tablet for that headache." He patted my lowered head.

"Thank you, sir."

I'd never felt so low. Nicola's rejection hurt deeply, and I couldn't understand why we had to fritter away what little time we had left with damp-eyed drama. I understood Nicola's worries about SIB, but we had only two weeks left. So far, I hadn't seen any military police personnel on campgrounds, so what were the chances of being caught? She said she loved me, so why not be with me? I didn't want to be another Helena and Sandy with a long-distance relationship. I wanted Nicola now, while we still had time.

Luckily, my afternoon offered a little relief in the form of a high-powered hockey match with the PTI team. I loved having something that was all my own and not part of 1Coy. My PTI buddies were a hoot, and I looked forward to my training once I left Guildford. It was hard to stay depressed while running around a hockey pitch. Exercise always lifted my mood.

I came back to room two after the hockey game to find Mandy a ball of bouncing hysteria on her bed.

"I've done it!" she babbled.

"Done what?" My stomach turned cold. Before she could answer, a bellow came down the corridor from the stairwell leading to the NCO offices below.

"Taylor! Turner! In my office. Now!" It was Judy's best and angriest bellow. I went pale.

"You haven't," I said to Mandy.

She clamped her hand over her mouth and burst into a fit of hysterical giggles. "The tea leaves. I did it," she squeaked.

For a moment, I thought she'd lost her mind.

"But she won't know until she gets ready for afternoon duty," Mandy added, "so she must want us for something else. Look at your face, Penny. Oh, we are a pair."

"Look at *my* face?" What planet was this girl living on? There was no time to bodily assault her. When Judy howled like a banshee, everyone moved at double-quick time.

Timidly, we entered her office and took up a stand-easy position before her desk. She was looking out the window with her back to us. My face fell. She was dressed in No2s, her parade dress. Her forage cap lay on the desk before us.

She didn't speak. I hated when she didn't speak much more than when she did. Mandy kept flitting me nervous glances, and I stared stonily ahead, refusing to acknowledge her. I was furious. I had been lassoed into another mess because of her infantile reaction to authority. This was a serious mess. This could be seen as assault, putting my career on the line.

Judy swung around so suddenly, she startled me, but part of that was the tea running down the side of her face to her chin, where little droplets dripped down the front of her uniform. The front of her uniform was stained. I felt faint and focused on the desktop, trying to keep my balance. Beside me, Mandy sniggered, actually sniggered. I could hardly believe my ears. It was soft, but in the stone-cold silence of Hacker's office, it sounded like the explosive crack before the avalanche. I braced myself and cursed the day I'd ever met Mandy. I should have left her at Guildford station. The mutton brain would probably still be sitting there on her stupid suitcase.

"Something amusing you, Turner?" Judy spoke, silky soft, like a cobra rustling through long grass. Even Mandy sensed the danger.

"N-No, Corporal."

"What about you, Taylor, do you find this funny?"

"No, Corporal. Not at all, Corporal."

"What's so interesting on my desk, then?"

"Nothing, Corporal."

"Eyes front!"

I snapped my head up and looked in detail at her face, with tea leaves dotted randomly here and there across her cheeks. I was so terrified, I worried I'd giggle with nerves. That would get me killed. I just knew it. She'd send me out to clean a minefield with a toothbrush or something.

"Of course, I can't prove this was you," she continued in the cobra voice.

Me? But it wasn't me.

"But where there's a stink, you're never far from it. So, rest assured, proof or not, you two...you two are going to suffer before I'm through with you."

Beside me, Mandy twitched. I wondered if she'd become somehow addicted to this torment.

"Return to your room. Get out!" Judy roared, making us jump.

We stumbled out into the corridor and blindly made our way toward the stairs to our floor. If I could legally have kept running, I would have, but that was called AWOL.

"That wasn't so bad," Mandy said, taking a big breath and looking around contentedly. "I thought we were let off light."

I grabbed her by the scruff of the neck as if she were a cur and shook her. She was as tall as I was, but I still managed to get her onto her tiptoes and rattle her brain.

"Let me make this perfectly plain," I snarled. "You were let off light. I, on the other hand, am being punished for something I did not do and had no part of. Next time you come up with a fucking stupid idea, don't come near me with it. Don't talk to me about it. In fact, keep out of my fucking way. Get my drift?"

"Oi, you two. I told you to get to your room!" Judy shouted from her office door. I let Mandy drop and stormed off, wondering how much Judy had heard, and how much she cared. I decided she didn't. She'd disliked me from the start and, to be honest, it was mutual. Except she had all the power.

Chapter 13

I fumed all the next day, and Mandy kept well out of my way. Here we were, on the brink of our sixth and last week, and she had basically learned nothing. News of the tea leaves exploit travelled on the camp grapevine like wildfire. Everywhere I went, I was either given coy looks of approval, or censorious frowns. Neither fitted my mood.

I'd an appointment at the hairdresser's, a very popular place just before a Passing Out day, since everyone wanted to look their best for visiting family and friends. On the way to the NAAFI, where the hairdresser worked, I saw Nicola coming toward me from the opposite direction. I slowed down, my heart hammering in my chest.

"Private Taylor." Nicola stopped to talk.

I was surprised, since she used to be so covert about us meeting out. Meeting anywhere, really. Maybe now that there was no "us," she could behave differently.

"I heard about the tea leaves," she said. Her eyes were cold.

"Oh." My face fell. I hadn't realised how stupid the hopeful smile I'd plastered all over it looked until it slid onto my shirt.

"Penny," she began in a softer tone, "That daft behaviour is exactly why we can't be together. Hacker is after your blood. She'll bring you down any way she can. People like her can bring us *all* down as surely as SIB can, and still you can't see the danger and pull stupid stunts like that."

"It wasn't me." The bleat was painful, even to my ears.

"Oh, Penny," she said sadly and brushed past me.

As I shuffled on toward the hairdresser's, tears blurred my vision, and I couldn't go in until I'd blinked them all away. It made me late for my appointment.

Sharon, the hairdresser, wasn't pleased at my tardiness, but gossip about my supposed exploits had put her in a good mood. She hated Judy—yet another one. A surprising number of people did, I was finding out.

"So, what are we going to do with this?" She ran her fingers through my shoulder-length dark hair. "Have you ever thought of highlights? It's the new big thing." Her fingers fluttered across my cheeks and forehead, chasing stray curls. I began to brighten. I liked being touched and appreciated. Also, who'd want to sit for hours in front of a mirror looking at a mopey mug like mine? Certainly not me.

Sharon was a hoot and soon had me laughing. Plus, she gave me coffee. I enjoyed her attentions, and halfway though, realised she was flirting with me. Sharon was flirtatious by nature, so I'd no idea if this meant she was gay. It didn't really matter. She made me feel good about myself at a time when I needed it most. My shorter, highlighted hairdo also cheered me up immensely.

When I left Sharon's with less hair and even less money, there was a new spring in my step and resolve in my heart. My feelings for Nicola were done with, locked away somewhere. Maybe one day I would bring them out and examine them, but only after a long, long time. For now, they were stored well out of reach.

It felt freeing to chuck out the heartache and I wondered why I hadn't done so earlier. I decided to never put myself through that sort of pain again. Losing Jackie had been hard, but it had a kind of purity or innocence to the loss—a coming of age. Nicola? Nicola had opened up a storm of heartfelt emotion in me. She'd brought love and lust and rawness with her. She cut deep.

In the end, it was a simple decision. The people SIB caught were long-term couples, people who eventually gave themselves away with their repeated patterns and sheep's eyes for one another. I, on the other hand, would have hundreds of simple shags and never be caught. I'd be the Scarlett Pimpernel of leslibeins! I laughed inwardly at my mother's old word fumble and felt a pang of homesickness. I'd be seeing her in a few days at our POP. She and Ted were coming down for it, and I felt inordinately happy and proud about that. I looked forward to showing them around my camp.

As I was near the NAAFI, I decided to detour and telephone my mother. It was hit or miss if she would be in.

"Taylor coal and coke merchants, how may I help you?" she answered in her poshest voice. She'd never liked using the phone, though she'd been as pleased as punch when Ted got it installed. They'd been the first in the street to have one.

"It's me, Mam," I said jauntily.

"Is everything all right?" She fell into her regular voice, but couldn't hide the anxiety in it. Why is it mothers always think something bad has happened when you're only calling on a whim?

"Everything's great. I just felt like calling you. Are you all set for Thursday?"

"Well..." The minute her voice changed, I knew what was coming. "Ted says he can't make it after all, so Peter and Mary are bringing me down. Christine and Alan are coming, too, and Kenny asked if he could come as well. Is that all right, love?"

Two things threw me. One, she'd called me "love," and two, who was Kenny? I went with the latter question.

"Who's Kenny?"

"Alan's brother. You met him at the wedding. He's asked after you a few times."

I frowned. Kissy Kenny, ick.

"Okay." I sounded dubious, and I was. "Well...I suppose it's okay. Someone might as well have Ted's seat." *Seeing as Ted's arse won't be in it.* I squashed down the disappointment.

Despite my mam's news, the rest of the day brightened—to match my new hairdo. I got compliments everywhere I went and began to ignore the censorious looks. I was not to blame for "Hacker's hatful," as the incident had become known. I had no reason to feel ashamed, even if I was going to be punished for it anyway. Lord only knew what Judy had lined up for me tomorrow, so I decided to hit the NAAFI bar that night with my new hair and footloose attitude. I knew tons of people now, so I didn't have to rely on someone from 3Plat as a wingman. In fact, I sat for a pint with a few of my new PTI mates until, on my way back from the loo, I met Vicky, the RP guard.

"Can I have a word?" She nodded to the door. I thought we were going outside, but instead she headed up the stairs to the recreational rooms. Whatever she wanted to say must be pretty private.

She led me to a room at the back that I hadn't seen before. It was used for storage and had chairs and tables piled up in one corner.

"What's up?" I asked.

She perched her hip on one of the tables. "I heard you and Nicola split up."

"We were barely together for more than three weeks," I said. I worked to keep the bitterness out of my voice. Vicky was one of Nicola's friends, so maybe she'd been sent along for a chat.

Vicky shrugged. So, she wasn't an ambassador for me getting back with Nicola, then.

"Is it true, about the tea leaves?" Vicky suddenly changed direction and wrong-footed me.

"No. And I'm tired of talking about that." I was. Well and truly tired. It was fine to be some sort of rebel today, and I suspected that's what Mandy got off on, but it was always followed by being tomorrow's chump, and that was the bit I didn't want to think about. At least not tonight. Tonight was all about distraction.

"Did you really bring me up here to talk about that?" I moved closer. If this wasn't about Nicola, it could only be about one other thing. I'd seen the way Vicky looked at me.

I sank my fingers in her curly blonde hair and pulled her into a fierce kiss. She melted against me like butter. I'd guessed right. Regimental Policewoman Vicky was up for it. My fingers wriggled up the back of her track top to reach her bra clasp. It gave at once and I cupped her small breasts. Her nipples were long and scratchy in the palms of my hands and suddenly touching them wasn't enough. I wanted to see them, to lick and suck. I pushed her top higher and laid her back on the tabletop. Vicky was compliant, happy to let me take the lead, and I realised that's what I needed this time. I wanted some power back, and this was how I would get it. I'd fuck Vicky senseless on a table. Simple as that.

Vicky whimpered and that fired me up all the more. I sucked her little tits hard. Her nipples were amazing, dark and long, and I nipped them with my teeth until she squealed, hanging on the threshold of pain and pleasure.

"You better keep quiet," I muttered. I was in no mood for an interruption. I'd been pent up since my last *coitus interruptus* with Nicola, and now Vicky was going to reap the benefit.

Her nails wracked my scalp, wrecking two quid's worth of hairdo, but I didn't mind. I kissed down her belly and played with her belly button while I tugged her track bottoms down around her ankles. Vicky's pubic hair was sparse but as blonde as the hair on her head. Her sex was small and tidy. Thin labia with a cheeky little clit that peeked out and winked at me. I ran my tongue over the length of her and she squirmed silently like a good girl. Then, I dove in, my tongue lashing her clitoris, and burrowed as deep as I could go. She began grunting, soft little sounds, her backside slapping up and down on the table. Vicky was close, and I decided to go for it rather than mess around trying to draw her out. I pursed my lips around her clit and sucked like hell while pushing two fingers into her as far as I could go and pumping her like fury. She gave a strangled scream and flooded the palm of my hand with her come. Her wetness, and the scream she hadn't managed to stifle, startled me.

We froze, straining to hear if anyone would check out the noise. Downstairs, the jukebox played "Didn't I (Blow Your Mind This Time)" by the Delfonics. Apart from that, the only other noise I could hear was the murmur of drinkers' voices. All seemed normal. We'd gotten away with it.

I stood and swapped places with Vicky, dropping my pants while she pulled hers up.

"Quick," I panted. I needed relief. Vicky dropped to

her knees without ceremony and buried her face in my sex. I was wet and ready to come. All I needed was a deft touch. Vicky hadn't one. She was very disappointing in the head department, almost timid. Her shy darting tongue failed to hit the mark and I had to slide my hand down between her face and my cunt and masturbate while she poked about like a blind dentist. I came. But it was no different from the wank I had most mornings in the shower. Vicky was a clueless lover. It was a pity, but I'd run out of time to teach her. I'd be leaving in a few days. I pulled up my pants and gave her a quick peck on the lips.

"I'd better go first," I said. "My mates will be wondering where I've got to."

She grabbed for my hand. "That was lush, Penny. Can we see each other again?"

"Well, you know I'm out of here soon. So, is it really worth it to upset Nicola? I mean, I'll be gone, and you'll be the one left here without your friend."

A flicker of hurt crossed Vicky's face, and I felt bad for her. But I'd told the truth, blunt as it was. What was she thinking, dragging me upstairs to a storeroom? That we'd have the greatest love affair of our lives? The army didn't work like that.

"Where were you?"

"I saw you talking to that RP."

The questions were waiting for me when I returned to my table, along with a flat pint of beer.

"Oh." I was fly on my feet. "She has a mate in Aldershot and wanted me to pass a message on. Now, whose round is it?" I asked.

"**P**rivate Taylor. Private Turner. So glad you could make it." Sarcastic Judy was as much a pain in the arse as apoplectic Judy. This would be bad. We were in her office, waiting to hear our fate.

"As you know, the Passing Out parade is this Thursday, and before that, we take part in the Platoon Cups. As Sergeant Manners has already explained," she continued in her saccharine voice. "The Accommodation Cup is very dear to her heart. I, therefore, think it's incredibly kind of you to volunteer to clean the common areas of this building, on all three floors...with scouring pads." She threw a box of Brillo pads at each of our heads. I caught mine. Mandy's bounced off, and she had to go scrambling across the floor after it.

"You begin tonight at 1800 and continue for each and every night until the job is done, top to bottom. I'll be popping in from time to time to see how you're progressing."

It was a very public and humiliating punishment, and I hated her more than ever. But maybe not as much as I hated Mandy, who was currently a sag-bag of self-pity beside me. I was glad I'd gone to the NAAFI bar the previous night, since there was no way I'd be going there again this week.

That evening, at 1800 hours, we heaved ourselves up the stairs to start at the door of Judy's private room and work our way down to the main door. It would take forever.

"I'm sorry, Penny." Mandy sniffled.

"Don't speak to me," I snapped. "In fact, go away. Start over at ablutions, and we'll meet at the stairwell and begin on the stairs."

Mandy sloped off. I was glad. I didn't want to listen to her prattling as she tried to make good of a stinking situation. I wanted to be alone with my own sad thoughts. Thoughts of Nicola and her sweet smile and French kisses, and...and in all honesty, what might have been.

It took two gruelling nights to scour the entire block's common areas. My hands were red raw, and to add to the humiliation, everyone had to pass by us and witness our degradation. It soon stopped any misplaced hero worship people had for us, and I hoped that sank in with

Mandy. Not that I saw that much of her. We barely spoke. I made her work on the opposite end of the building, and at night, though our bunks were side by side, I was so knackered that I fell into bed and ignored her.

Once, as I was crawling along the corridor like a cockroach, a pair of well-polished shoes stopped directly before me. I looked up expecting to see Judy again. She'd passed by a few minutes before with a few of her NCO buddies, no doubt clawing back her dignity by displaying me on my hands and knees. This time, Sgt Manners stood over me. She gave me a hard, thin-lipped look.

"You have the makings of a good soldier, Taylor," she snapped. "I suggest you think long and hard about who you hang out with on your next deployment." It turned out to be the best advice I ever received in the army. With that, she marched off. At least she didn't stomp all over the patch I'd just cleaned, like Judy's mates had done.

Competition week arrived and we were as jittery as hell.

Monday began with the physical training competition. For most platoons, this was the easiest cup of all. Twenty minutes of synchronised exercise. To me it was a breeze. I could do this all day. But 3Plat had a lot of lazy arses that I knew would suffer after even five minutes of hopping about. Nevertheless, Cpl Bury did her best for us. She hid the real problem kids at the rear and put me, Doreen, and anyone else remotely fit to the front.

From the front, I couldn't see how the girls behind were performing. Manners sat at the judges' table with the other senior ranks, and not once did a flicker of a smile cross her crab-apple face. Manners didn't believe in encouragement, while Bones smiled and encouraged us continuously, keeping us motivated and in sync.

Our stint over, we shuffled back to the locker room to change while 4Plat marched in to begin their torture session. Once the competition ended, all four platoons marched back into the gym and stood at ease before the judges.

Major Travis, who had welcomed me to her PTI fold only a few weeks before, stood to announce the winner. "I'm Major Travis, head of ASPT, Aldershot." She gave a cheery smile. I liked Travis. She was human, a thing not necessarily guaranteed by a uniform. "I've enjoyed today's sport immensely. You have all performed to a high standard and I'm pleased with the work my PTIs have obviously put into your training." A little huzzah for her own people there, always a sign of a good officer.

"It has, therefore, been a very difficult decision, and, unfortunately, there has to be only one winner. After what I've seen this afternoon, there are no losers in this gym right now. You were all brilliant." She started applauding us, and everybody immediately joined in. What a lovely woman.

The applause faded away and she continued, "So, which platoon should win the cup? That's what I had to decide, and decided I have." Manners's face tightened. This cup did mean something to her, despite her earlier protestations. Travis brandished the trophy. "I'm pleased to announce that the winners of the PT Cup are 3 Platoon."

There was silence. We were stunned. Then Manners jumped to her feet, punched the air, and gave a war whoop of delight. We joined in the impromptu celebration and slapped each other's backs with relief. The other platoons were a sea of glum faces. I pitied them for later, especially if they had sergeants like Manners. But, then, who knew what waited around the corner for us. Would one cup be enough to appease her?

"Look at Manners's smile," whispered Carol. "Did you ever think you'd see the day?"

"Let's hope one cup is enough," I replied. "But I doubt it."

The Commandant, Colonel St. John-Powell, presented

the cup, and Manners, with great largesse, beckoned to Bones to receive it on 3Plat's behalf.

That night was an In-night, which I found spiteful considering we'd just won a cup and should be allowed to go celebrate. But as Mo pointed out, this was so we could blitz our floor in preparation for the Accommodation Cup.

When Manners had previously upended our rooms, we'd done a good job of dusting them down and repacking our kit. We'd also pulled all the furniture out and washed down the walls. There was no way Manners was going to catch us out again, though she'd have been mad to make a mess this close to the Accommodation Cup inspection. She did do a spot inspection the next morning while we were off to breakfast, and upon seeing that all our things were in place when we got back, we assumed we'd passed muster. Not that Manners had one word of praise to say about it, anyway.

Instead, we were marched out to the parade square and made to practice our drill while St. John-Powell and the platoon officers inspected every block in turn.

Marching up and down in our little quadrant, 4Plat swished along like a Singer sewing machine. They were all straight lines and well-oiled arm swings. The Drill Cup was definitely theirs. *Que sera sera*, as Doris Day said. I accepted that this cup was not going anywhere near us, and relaxed and swung my own arms about a bit, too. Just to show off.

From the corner of my eye, I noticed the Commandant and her entourage heading over the parade square toward us. The Accommodation inspection was over. We were marched back to the drill hut with the other platoons to wait. Meanwhile, the camp Commandant and her senior officers lined up on the stage, which was set up at the head of the square for our Passing Out parade. Once the senior officers were ready, we were all marched back out, 1Plat leading and 4Plat bringing up the rear.

"Company, company halt. Stand at ease!" the sergeant major bellowed.

"I have inspected your accommodation," the Commandant began, "and, as usual, I was impressed by the high standard. I normally have a difficult time judging the winners, but this time there is no doubt in my mind who the winning platoon is. From the moment I walked onto their floor, I could see how much work had gone into their cleanliness. I could sense high standards. I could sense platoon unity. It was obvious that this platoon had worked hard together to achieve such an amazing standard. It gives me great pleasure in announcing that the winner of the Accommodation Cup is...3 Platoon."

We wanted to cheer, but we were on parade and couldn't.

"Three Platoon!" Judy stepped forward. "Three Platoon, 'shun. One step forward. March!"

Sgt Manners marched forward to personally take the cup off the Commandant. They saluted each other. Manners turned around as Judy ordered, "Three platoon. One step back. March. Stand at ease."

Manners raised the cup above her head, and we finally cheered our lungs out.

The final competition, and the big one, was the Drill Cup.

It started the next day at 1000 hours. St. John-Powell, as Commandant, was taking the salute. God, but I was nervous. We'd been practising in secret for weeks, but would it be enough? Four Plat were red-hot contenders, but we could strut our stuff to "Rose Garden" real fancy, though it wasn't really the same thing.

The competition worked through each platoon in numerical order, which meant Sgt Meeke's 1Plat went first.

They were still a mess and thankfully set a low standard. The rest of us loitered nervously in the drill hut while Meeke thundered through the commands outside.

Eventually, Manners called, "Three platoon, 'shun. About turn."

This got us into order while 2Plat stomped up their dust next. We waited for the March order. I stared at Manners, assuming there'd be some words of encouragement. The other platoon sergeants had given them. Even Meeke had dug deep and found a platitude for her bunch of losers. Manners's attention was elsewhere, awaiting a signal of her own to move her platoon onto the parade ground. It came, and she straightened that extra inch. We, as a unit, straightened a little extra, too, in sync with her. She turned to us and ordered, "Three Platoon. To the tune of "Rose Garden," by the left. By the right. Quick march!"

I nearly tripped over my "by the left" foot, and I couldn't have been the only one. She knew! She knew about our secret practise sessions! I felt supercharged. I forgot it was the Commandant taking the salute, and my nerves simply deserted me, leaving behind a kind of euphoria. The rest of 3Plat responded similarly. We were parading on clouds of pride, not tarmacadam.

Our squad was marching well, without the inevitable

shuffle of feet that went with a lost step. I felt proud and I really didn't care anymore if we won or lost this one. Two cups were more than enough. Suddenly, it wasn't about a competition. This was about being a soldier. Being a platoon in Her Majesty's Armed Forces.

By the end of the competition, we were all back in the drill hut as 4Plat finally filed in. We were all bundles of excited nerves. The sergeant major arrived. No rest for the wicked, or the elated.

"One Coy. Ten'shun! Squad will move to the right in threes. Right turn," she commanded, and took us back across the parade square. "By the left. Quick march. Right wheel." She halted us in front of the Commandant.

"I'm not going to waste time." The Commandant began a very quick speech. "There was one platoon in particular that marched with flair and determination. This platoon has shone throughout all their training. There is no shame on the other platoons, but 3 Platoon have won yet again. Congratulations."

"Three Platoon!" Manners ordered. "Three Platoon, 'shun. One step forward. March!"

Lt Perryman, our senior officer, marched forward to receive the cup. She held the cup above her head and we cheered. Then we joined the rest of the company and marched back to our accommodation.

"I don't know how you lot did it, but you were great out there," Judy said grudgingly, once we were at ease before Block B.

"I know how," Manners marched up the slope to join us. "I was very proud when I saw you practising all those nights." She looked us straight in the eye. "I've never seen such a determined platoon. I don't know who was behind the extra drill practise, but I'm very proud of each and every one of you." She puffed up like a little bantam hen. "But, did you have to pick *that* bloody song? *I hate it!*"

Chapter 14

The big day dawned. The 1Coy Passing Out parade. My mother, Pete and Mary, Cousin Christine and her new hubby, Alan, along with last-minute Kenny, turned up in their Sunday best and were shown to their seats in the spectator stands. The sun was shining and the breeze was just enough to keep the Union Jacks snapping over everyone's heads.

I was so looking forward to marching with the band. I wished we'd had a chance to do it earlier. Memories of 2Coys POP came flooding back and the thrum of the military band had me tingling again all over.

The band of the Women's Royal Army Corps led the march with "The Lass of Richmond Hill." We followed behind in numerical platoon order as usual. As we marched past the crowds, I tried to get a glimpse of my family but there were too many people and rubbernecking wasn't an option.

After the parade, we stood to attention as the Commandant inspected us. Then, she made a long-winded speech and announced the competition cup winners. I felt proud of my platoon and of myself. On each win announcement, we were brought to attention while Lt Perryman, 3Plat SO, marched forward to receive the cups all over again. I knew my family were witnessing all of this and pushed down the little pang that Ted had decided not to come. He'd have been proud, the stupid bastard.

After the ceremony, we were free to entertain our friends and families, who were allowed to visit our accommodation blocks.

"How's it been?" my mother asked, even though I'd called her every other week and kept her up to date—with the good news, of course.

"A piece of cake." I smiled. "It's a pity Ted couldn't make it."

I expected her to cover up for him, and was surprised when she said, "He's missed out on one of the best days of his life."

Mam was impressed by our accommodation—especially how tidy my room was. "Never knew you had it in you." She sniffed, then smiled.

"Let's go get a drink." I took her arm and we went in search of my cousin Christine and the others.

Kenny had been hovering around me like a fly all afternoon. Eventually, he collared me at the NAAFI bar.

"Can I have a minute?"

"Sure." I took him outside and lit a cigarette. I remembered the last time I'd seen him, I'd sworn off the things. So much for willpower.

"I've bought you a little present," he said, sheepishly.

"You what?" I regarded him suspiciously.

He gave me a little black jewellery box. Inside, nestled among black crepe, was a silver pendant. A lapis lazuli stone mounted on a silver disc. It was simple but pretty. Not too ornate, and I liked it immediately.

"Thanks, Kenny. It's lovely," I said in surprise and began to put the box in my pocket. "Is this for my Passing Out?" I was confused. My immediate family hadn't brought me a present, so why had Kenny?

"No, not for Passing Out." He looked upset that I'd put it away so quickly.

"Not allowed with the uniform," I explained, though I'd no idea if that was true or not. "Thank you again." I reached up and gave him a little peck on the cheek.

He turned scarlet and blurted, "I want you to be my girlfriend."

I was shocked. "Can I think about it? After all, you're almost family." I flapped, looking for excuses.

"No, we're not." He scoffed. Obviously, he'd thought about that one. "You're only Christine's cousin." He shrugged awkwardly. "For sure, think about it." We began to head back to the bar and he held the door open for me. "But don't take too long, okay?"

I could have told him the answer that very minute, a big fat "no," but why spoil a lovely day? I didn't want Kenny's gloomy face hanging around. This was my big day with my family and I didn't want it hijacked. I'd write him a letter later.

A marquee stood on the green for the visitors to partake of a light lunch. It was the best food I'd tasted in six weeks, apart from my short stay in the MRS. I stopped that train of thought immediately, and instead listened to Christine complain about how we were too well fed. The afternoon was relaxed and a little boozy, and visitors had to be off base for 1800 hours. I gave my mam, Pete, Mary, and Christine a big kiss. Alan got a peck on the cheek and, after a second of deliberation, I did the same for Kenny, with a well-aimed look. It sank in, and he left with the rest of them, in a mild sulk. They'd booked into a little hotel in Guildford, and for them the night would continue with a few more glasses in the hotel bar. Me, I had similar plans, except down at the NAAFI. Now I could shuck off my uniform, put on my best civvies, and let the party begin.

When I got there, the jukebox was on full volume and the floor was sticky with spilled beer. The place was rammed as the WRAC band was heading off to Germany later that evening, so it was a double session.

Mandy, me, and Doreen piled onto the little square of a dance floor to "Knock Three Times" by Tony Orlando and Dawn. Everyone knew the words to the chorus and all hell broke loose every time it came around, with everyone banging their glasses three times on their tables.

I felt a tap on my shoulder and turned around to come face to face with Nicola. She looked wonderful in a slinky blue dress that matched her eyes. She leaned in and shouted in my ear, "I just wanted to say congratulations."

"What?" I cupped my ear and pretended not to hear her. In reality, I was sucking in the warmth of her body and the smell of Charlie perfume.

"Congratulations."

I knew I could push it a little further, so I grabbed her by the elbow and pressed a way for us through the crush. She let me lead her when she could have broken away, and I took that as a good sign.

"Thank you," I said when we finally found a peaceful enough place by the front door. It was open, to allow in fresh air, and the cool breeze was welcome after the crush of bodies. We were still in a public place, though.

I wasn't sure how far I could take this. "Did you hear we won the cups? All of them."

Nicola laughed. "Yes, I did. I wasn't surprised. You're something special, Penny. You make things happen." Her eyes were laced with a sad, fierce pride. She really did love me. I could see it clearly and my heart hiccupped.

"I couldn't make us happen," I said softly, checking that no one could overhear.

Nicola's lip twisted into a rueful smile. "I'm not sure you were totally committed to the idea."

"That's not fair."

"Isn't it?"

I shut up then, since it was true. My exploits with Vicky made that clear, even to me. I wasn't sure how much Nicola knew about Vicky. I hadn't done anything wrong—we had split by that point—but I'd rather she didn't find out, either.

"Can I see you before I go?" I asked. "I'm for Aldershot next week." Well, talking to Bones, I'd assumed I'd be, though so far, I'd heard nothing official.

"I'm on leave from tomorrow," she said.

"What? For how long?"

"A week. I'm going home for a visit."

My face fell. It never occurred to me Nicola would be gone before I would. "I'll miss you." And it was true. I hated goodbyes, and I hated this stupid rushed one most of all.

"Follow me." Nicola seemed to make her mind up about something and moved off at a quick pace.

We crossed the green to a set of accommodation blocks on the other side of the base. I knew this was the band block, though I'd never been in it before. Nicola led me down a corridor on the ground floor to the back of the block. We entered a single room.

"Whose room is this?" I looked around in interest. It was small, but someone had made it homey, with soft cushions, a radio, and a bright bed throw.

"A friend in the band let me borrow it. I share mine." Nicola turned and gave me a searing kiss.

My knees began to tremble. She had such power over me. A power no one else seemed to have. Did that make this love? Was I in love?

"Why do you need to do that?" I mumbled, my brain dissolving. "Borrow a room?"

Nicola pulled back and began to undo my jeans. "I needed it in case I wanted to seduce you tonight."

"Oh?" I began to fumble with the zipper on the back of her dress. "What made you think I'd be that easy?" My jeans hit the tops of my shoes. Nicola shimmied her dress over her shoulders and it landed in a silky puddle on the floor.

"This," she said and gently pushed me backward. With my pants around my ankles, I fell on top of the bed. In only a matching lace bra and panties, Nicola crawled over me, tugging my tee shirt up over my bra. I hurried to help her remove my last few pieces of clothing until I lay naked underneath her.

"I love you," I blurted, not at all romantically. I'd always thought when I finally said it, there'd be roses and wine and moonlight and...and maybe caviar, though I'd never had caviar. But I was willing to give it a go on a special night for that special someone. And here I was with my jeans wrapped around my shoes, lying naked across a strange soldier's bed. Love was bizarre.

"These last few weeks have been hell," I said earnestly.

She kissed my neck, along my collarbone, and moved slowly down to my breasts. I gasped. Her lips were cool and soft, and I buried my hands in her hair when she licked a nipple.

Her hands brushed across my belly in slow massaging circles building up an intense warmth that spread down to my aching thighs. I tried to guide her hand lower, but she pulled away with a soft tut. Slowly, she slid off the bed until she was kneeling on the floor between my legs. She spread me and took her time in the mellow lamplight to examine my response to her lovemaking. I was wet and ready, and she carefully placed the broad of her tongue against my labia and began stroking me slowly. I undulated under her like water rippling over sand, slowly rising to meet her. She took her time and masterfully built me up and left me cresting on the edge of a huge orgasm. Then, she narrowed her tongue like a spear and plunged it into me repeatedly as I jerked under her, crying out my pleasure. It was deep and intense, and it shook me in a way I'd never felt before.

When I could draw breath, I pulled her to me and we lay sprawled across the bed. She wiped my tears away.

"What's wrong, baby?" she whispered.

"I love you." This time, I said it right and found I didn't need caviar and all the props. I simply needed her. She drew the bed covers over us and cuddled me tight. I was exhausted after such an emotional day. But I knew she cared for me. Nicola was so right for me. She smelled right, she tasted right. She...she was...the one for...

"Penny. Penny. Wake up, for God's sake! You need to get back to your block, pronto!"

"Huh?" I rolled over, squinting at the bright overhead light. Where had my mellow lamplight gone? Where had Nicola gone? What was Debs doing here shouting at me?

"Nicola?" I sat up, dragging the bedclothes to cover my nakedness.

"She's gone." Debs tossed me my jeans and kicked a shoe in my direction. "Get dressed. You've got to get out of here."

"Gone where?"

"To her own bed, I should think, as should you."

"But... What time is it?" I looked around for a clock as I slowly dragged my tee shirt back on. I'd been lying on it and it was a creased mess.

"You're twenty minutes late for your curfew, you'll be roasted if they find you."

That sped me up. I pulled on my jeans and stuffed my knickers and bra in my pockets.

"Nicola—" I started again, but Debs cut me short.

"Nicola has gone. She told me to tell you to get lost. You need to get back to your room. That's all there is to know, Penny."

"But Nicola loves me."

Debs found my other shoe under the dressing table and tossed it over. "That may well be."

"And I love her." I shoved my feet into my shoes without bothering to undo the laces, at the same time realizing I was well and truly pissed. I could barely stand straight. "We made up tonight."

"Is that so?" I began to focus on Debs's face. It was hard, all angles and sharp edges under the harsh overhead light. She was angry. Why was she here—this wasn't her room, was it? And if it was, then she must have known what was going to happen. Was she angry Nicola and I had sex? What did she think we were going to do, play Scrabble?

"Is this your room?" I asked, confused at her anger. I was confused about everything, truth be told.

"No. Now get out of here. I have to fix this place back the way it was." The sharpness in Debs's voice gave something away. This was her girlfriend's room, and she was proprietary about it.

"Okay, I'm going, I'm going. It was Nicola brought me here in the first place." God, but it was hard enough to stand, never mind concentrate. "Where is Nicola?" I asked again, looking around stupidly as if she might jump out of the wardrobe laughing.

Debs lost patience. "Maybe you should go talk to Vicky," she said angrily. "She and Nicola had a long conversation this afternoon."

I stood there slack-jawed until Debs took my arm and roughly led me to the door. "You need to go, Penny. Your time here is over, both at Guildford and in Nicola's life. You had your chance and you blew it!" She shoved me out in the corridor and snapped the door shut on my confused face.

There was nothing I could do. I had to get back to Block B as fast as possible, and hopefully unseen. God only knew the barrage of questions waiting for me there. I stumbled across camp, keeping away from the streetlights, blending into to the darker corners. My head was whirling. Nicola loved me. I had seen it. She had said it. You can't fake things like that. And I loved her. I could see that now. I did, I really did. As much as I was ever able to.

Damn Vicky and her blabbermouth. Damn Debs, too. I hadn't meant to hurt Nicola. They were all wrong about me.

My block came into view up the hill, and I began to run toward it. Somewhere behind me, in a room I didn't know because I could never be invited there, was Nicola. In the morning, she'd go on leave, and I'd be stuck here until my deployment. I wouldn't see her go, wouldn't have the chance to say sorry, or even goodbye. Nicola, however, had already said her goodbye. It was in every kiss, every caress she had given me. I knew that now.

I wanted to cry but I wouldn't let myself. I was a soldier, and a damn good one. And somehow, I'd put this behind me if I was to survive as a lesbian in Her Majesty's Army.

Chapter 15

The next morning, we gathered in our platoon office while Lt Perryman, 2Coy's OC, handed out envelopes with our new postings. I was dog-tired and emotionally all over the place, but the excitement of my fellow 'toonies soon seeped under my skin and overthrew my self-defeated mood.

Once Perryman left, we unceremoniously ripped our envelopes open. Joan was off to be a driver at Catterick and Carol was for the Intelligence Corps—no surprises there, since she was made for that posting. Mandy had decided to be a stewardess and was posted here at Guildford. Somehow, this didn't surprise me. She'd been a waitress at a Wimpy Bar back home before joining the army, and the best she could come up with after six weeks training was to continue as an all-round dogsbody, only in a different uniform. Her reputation as a troublemaker would have her washing dishes for eternity.

I'd never fully understand Mandy, and that was fine because I knew what *I* wanted, and I was heading for

Aldershot and the ASPT course in...bloody hell. I reread the letter.

I had a week to go before my course began. Meantime, I, along with several others, was to report to Holding and Drafting in Guildford until called upon.

Corporal Burns was waiting for us at H&D. "It never fails to surprise me who washes up on these shores." She was a pal of Judy's and gave me a particularly hard look. We were allocated rooms and given individual appointments with Captain Peters, the commanding officer of H&D. Mine was one of the first, and I found it not only uncomfortable, but a real eye-opener.

"So, you're the infamous Taylor we've all heard so much about," was her opening line when she finally decided to look up from her paperwork. "Seems you've made a bit of a name for yourself," she continued in a quiet, dry voice.

Peters didn't scream like most of the other officers. She terrified with intensity. There was a pause that I was expected to fill, but I didn't know what to say.

She gave an owlish blink at my lack of response and said, "I will not tolerate any bad attitude at H&D. You will do guard duty on Saturday and Sunday. On Monday, you start five days' leave, and on return, you'll be back on weekend guard duty. Understand?"

This was to keep me out of trouble. I felt reprimanded, as well as belittled, and a spike of anger at Mandy tore through me. It would take forever for the stink of her misdemeanours to fade and I realised I, too, was tainted, and I couldn't completely blame Mandy for all of it.

"Yes, ma'am."

"Dismissed."

Back in my room, I met my new roommates. Sharon was a pretty blonde with a prominent scar on her left temple. It added a roguishness that she knew damn well how to play. Patty was perhaps the butchest-looking woman on camp, but she was very popular and likeable—a big softy with an infectious laugh. I took to them immediately, and the little butterflies of anxiety that had been building all morning began to melt away.

"Hi, I'm Penny," I said.

"Oh, we know who you are, all right," Sharon said. It wasn't bitchy, but I felt uncomfortable that my name preceded me. I realised this was something I'd have to outgrow. I was no longer a troublemaker. I wanted to be good at my job. I was proud to be in the army and wanted the army to be proud of me.

Sharon and Patty took me under their wing for that initial first day and gave me a quick tour of H&D and the people in it. The queerness I had picked up on in my early visits to the NAAFI bar was not a mistake, and by dinner I had met at least a dozen lesbians and was amazed at how I seemed to instinctively know who was and wasn't "family."

Sharon led me into the cookhouse and for the first time, I crossed the divide to the permanent staff side of the canteen. It amused me that this used to be my Holy Grail. Now it was just as grimy as the other side. The other man's grass may not be greener but at least it had real milk and not that awful powdered stuff.

"A few of us are hitting the town on Friday night. Want to tag along?" she said.

"You bet." I couldn't wait to get off base with my new mates and have a drink and a dance. It would be refreshing to be away from the base and the NAAFI bar.

"Okay. Bring your glad rags. We get changed in the bushes behind Smokey Joe's." She named a greasy spoon joint along the Royal Mile.

"You what?"

Sharon smiled at my greenness. "You aren't allowed off base in trousers, so unless you like wearing a skirt, we all take our jeans and change in the bushes behind Smokey Joe's. It's private enough."

I saw this private dressing room up front and personal

that Friday night. It was exactly as Sharon said, a well-concealed spot behind the cafe, where the girls stripped off their skirts, stuffed them in a bag, and donned their Wranglers or Levi's, ready for a night out. The bushes were adorned with plastic bags with skirts and nylon tights in them. A little like nature's locker room.

The pub we were headed for was called The Seven Stars and it was a lesbian mecca. I recognized several faces from the camp from across many of the lower ranks. So, this was where Nicola and her mates hung out. Except Nicola was on leave this week. What a shame, we could have talked and tried to make amends... somehow. The way she'd left things between us gave me a bitter taste in my mouth that beer wouldn't wash away. Maybe a casual lover would?

I found one easily—a girl from Q store—and we made out in a toilet cubicle. I didn't bother to remember her name. I was tipsy and high on the elation of my new-found freedom, mixed with an irritating itch for Nicola that I knew I would never truly master.

Guard duty was as boring as it looked and was made much worse because now I knew my friends were heading for The Seven Sisters as they filed past me on

Saturday night. The only relief, such as it was, was that on Monday morning, I'd be headed home for five days' leave. My mam was excited, but I had mixed feelings.

The train ride up to Darlington put these feelings all into focus. I didn't fit into my old life anymore. I was a lesbian, and I'd have to hide it from my family. Before, throughout all my fumblings with, and hero worship of, Jackie, I'd never really considered who I was and what my immature feelings meant. Now I knew. As usual, when I had a free moment, my thoughts swung to Nicola. Did she feel this way when she went home? She'd be on her way back to camp now.

I wryly thought about how fate conspired to have us miss each other. Life was a revolving door, spewing us out in the wrong direction at the wrong time. I missed her. I also hated her, but mostly I missed her. Inside, I felt hollow and didn't know if something new had opened up or something old had simply disappeared. I did know I was unhappy and out of balance, and Nicola was the reason. From the moment I first saw her on in-oculation day, she had burned through me like a virus. Lovesick. That's what I was. I was a lovesick fool.

My mam waited for me on the platform while Ted sat in the car on the street. I felt disappointed he hadn't bothered to meet me on the platform, but Mam rushed to point out how horrendous the parking around the station was, as if she were a little disappointed in him, too, and felt the need to cover for him.

"What the hell have you done with your hair?" was his greeting to me as I climbed into his Ford Cortina. "It's a bloody mess."

"Nice to see you too, Ted."

"Meet any nice boys in Guildford?" Mam asked, as Ted manoeuvred the car out of his parking spot. Kenny must have told her about my "Dear John" letter.

"It's an all-female camp, Mam."

And so began my home leave.

By Friday afternoon, Guildford camp gates were a welcome sight. I couldn't wait to see everybody again and head down to the Seven Stars for a boozy catch-up. As my taxi turned onto Royal Mile, a Vauxhall Cresta military vehicle passed on the way out from the camp. An official army driver was driving it, but it was the uniform of the woman passenger that caught my attention. She had the red forage cap of the military police.

I paid my fare and walked the last few yards to the guardhouse to sign in, wondering who was on duty this

afternoon. I was very familiar with the ugly box struc-
ture by now and knew I'd find a bored buddy inside.

"Hi." I greeted Patty, my old butch roommate.

"Oh, my God!" She looked like she'd seen a ghost. I
laughed.

"It's only been a week."

"But...but..." She stared down the Royal Mile after
my taxi.

I turned to look along with her as my cab disappeared
around a corner. "I know. A little extravagant but I
missed you all so much I had to race over here from the
train station."

"Not that, you nob. SIB! They've just left."

I realised she meant the Cresta. "I know," I said con-
spiratorially. "I saw them. So, what's going on, what are
they doing snooping around here?" It was the first time
I'd laid eyes on our mysterious Aunt Sybil.

"Penny." Patty looked at me as if I was thicker than a
wet sheep. "They've gone to get you."

"What?"

"Nicola was investigated this week and has disappeared. She's not come back to camp."

I was stunned by this, but Patty's next words thrust a
knife into my stomach. "SIB were here looking for you."

Patty had no more news, she only knew the bare

bones of the story, so I lugged my gear as fast as I could over to my bunkroom at H&D, hoping to find someone who knew what the hell was going on. As it was lunchtime, the block was empty, so I dumped my stuff and ran to the cookhouse.

Cherie looked dumbfounded when she saw me enter. "What are you doing here?"

"Avoiding SIB, it seems." I went to sit with her. "What the hell is going on?"

Cherie immediately gathered together her half-eaten meal and stood. "Not here. There are too many spies. Follow me."

Spies? This freaked me out. She dumped her tray, and we headed outside.

"Where's Nicola?" I demanded as soon as we were alone. "Patty said she's not been seen since the investigation started."

"SIB arrived late Tuesday and searched Nicola's room while she was away on home leave. I heard they took letters from her knicker drawer, but I don't know if that's true or not," Cherie told me as we strolled across the green with no particular destination in mind. She looked tired and fretful and was obviously worried for her friend, as well as herself. Now my own fears came into play as I realised how vulnerable we all were.

"She's devastated, Penny," Cherie continued. "SIB went to her home to interview her. Imagine, in front of her parents and everything. Bastards."

"How do you know this?" According to Patty, SIB were on their way to find me. They knew I was on leave. Could they be knocking on my family's front door even now?

"She rang me while her parents were out," Cherie said. "We didn't have much time to talk, but she did tell me she's officially out of the army. Her parents have her in lockdown. They won't even let her out of the house."

"Oh, God." This was awful. Poor Nicola. "But why Nicola? Can they even search her room while she's not there?"

"Apparently, they can if there's been an official report. That's what I meant by spies. Someone shopped her in."

"Fuck." This was unimaginable. Then, a thought occurred. I'd missed a salient point in this flood of devastating news. "Letters. You said they found letters?"

Cherie shrugged. "I've no idea if that's true. Lieutenant Perryman escorted SIB during the search, but she's not saying anything."

"SIB's been back. Patty told me they were heading off to talk to me. I don't know if that's true either."

"You're a jammy bugger, Taylor. You missed them by the skin of your teeth."

"They'll catch up with me soon enough once they realise I came back and passed them on the way." I was thinking furiously. "I have to get my story straight. What I really need is to talk to Nicola. Does anybody have her home phone number?"

"It'll be on her file in company offices."

"Great." She might as well have said the North Face of Everest.

"Could still be your lucky day, Penny. It's Friday afternoon and the senior ranks normally piss off for the weekend." Out of the blue, she gave me a cheeky grin. "Have you reported to company offices yet?"

"Not yet. But—"

"Well, go now. CO is full of *family*."

I had an *ah-ha* moment and ran along as instructed. On the way there, I was conscious of being the attention of everyone I passed. No one said anything, but the flicker of an eye and a sly nudge to a companion said it all. The whole camp knew. I was a sweating ball of paranoia by the time I arrived at CO, where I was delighted to find Sharon, my new roommate behind the desk. Switched on as ever, she immediately took control as I genteelly unravelled before her. If SIB had walked through the door at that minute, I'd have fallen to my knees and confessed to anything.

"We need to get you booked in and back off camp before Sybil returns." Seeing I was beyond use, she mercifully took over the crisis management. I was amazed at how everyone seemed to know what was happening, yet, apparently, nobody was saying anything. This was the gay grapevine in action with military precision.

Sharon soon had all the paperwork ready and I was booked in and issued a forty-eight-hour pass within five minutes. "Where are you going to lay low, Penny?" she asked. "I know Sandy's house is booked out this weekend."

"I desperately need to speak to Nicola, but I don't know how to contact her."

Sharon began digging about in the filing cabinets and returned with Nicola's file. She scoured through it and eventually wrote down a London telephone number and address. "I never gave you this." She gave me a steely glare. "I'll already get it in the neck for the *mistake* with your leave pass. Okay?" I nodded in acknowledgment. I owed her my firstborn for this.

"Thank you. Thank you so much." I knew I had a real friend here, a *family* friend, and that galvanised me for what lay ahead.

"You've got until Monday to sort this shit out," Sharon said. This calmed me a little bit. I had breathing space, but it didn't resolve the problem. I still needed to speak to Nicola and, hopefully, we'd figure out how to deal with Sybil.

It was a desperate situation. My army career could be well and truly over, and I'd only been in it less than two months. I'd no idea where I could possibly go if I was discharged. The thought of going back to live in Darlington made me feel sick.

I ensured I had enough coins to feed the greedy NAAFI pay telephones, went through my story again in my head, and began to dial. My hands shook so badly, I misdialled several times before getting through.

"Hello?" a male voice answered, obviously Nicola's father.

"Oh, hello. Is it possible to speak to Nicola, please?"

"And who are you?"

"Oh, excuse me, this is Pearl, her friend from nursing school," I said in my poshest voice.

"May I ask what you want her for?" She really was in lockdown. I began to panic. What if I couldn't blag my way into seeing her?

"Well..." I hesitated enough to make him uneasy. "Well, she's my bridesmaid and we're shopping for dresses this weekend. Hasn't she said anything?" I put a mild hint of accusation into my tone, as if I was stressed out enough without all his questioning.

"Oh." He was confused now and that suited me just fine. What with all that had happened in his household recently, I'm sure he could imagine that a mundane matter like shopping with a girlfriend could get overlooked. "I'll get her for you now."

The phone clattered as he handed it over. "It's for you, someone called Pearl. You're going shopping with her tomorrow."

Then, I heard the sweet lilt of Nicola's voice. "Hello?" She sounded mystified.

"It's me." Tears welled in my eyes. It was so good to talk to her again. "I need to see you and I've a plan. I've told your dad you're my bridesmaid, and we went through nursing training together, and that—"

"Oh, hello, Pearl." Nicola caught on quick. "Sorry I haven't got back to you. I've been so busy." She put a lot of apology into her words. Clearly, her parents were close by, eavesdropping at her end. "Of course, I hadn't forgotten. How could I?" This sounded like a bad lie and it worked perfectly. I could hear a female murmur off to the side and assumed her mother was asking questions.

"I'm so sorry to hear what's happened to you," I said. I had no idea how long we had to speak before a parent stopped the call. "I need to see you this weekend. Sybil is coming back on Monday to interview me and—"

Whatever she relayed to her parents worked. "I agree," Nicola said, talking over me. "I'd love to come shopping with you." She sounded so much brighter. "Mum says we should look along Oxford Street. There's great shops there."

"I take it this is all going okay?" I asked allowing myself to relax a modicum. There came more murmuring somewhere offline.

"Yes," Nicola replied to all three of us, still playing her role as excited bridesmaid. Then, "What's that, Mum?" To me she said, a little breathlessly, "Mum says you should stay over so you don't have such a big trek back."

"You're joking."

"Pearl says yes, Mum, and thank you." I heard Nicola call over her shoulder to her mother. She was playing her part masterfully. "Yes. Eleven o'clock at Oxford Circus. I'll meet you there. Give my love to Brian."

"Who's Brian?" I asked bewildered.

"And tell him not to overdo it at the bachelor party," Nicola admonished, laughing. "See you tomorrow at one o'clock. Bye, Pearl." She hung up with a little kiss.

Apparently, Brian was my husband-to-be.

Nicola's mother looked just like her. It was a surprise to see her waiting for me alongside Nicola outside the Oxford Street entrance to the underground. I had been naïve to think that Nicola and I would have any real time together. Her parents were still highly protective and prohibitive of her. But looking at her thin, eager face, I was glad to be there and offer a bit of relief from the nightmare she was going through.

"Pearl."

"Nicola."

We hugged.

"You've lost weight!" I mentioned. It was true. She had barely enough on her bones as it was, and her weight loss was shocking. "And this must be your mother." I turned on the charm.

"Call me Wendy." Mrs Scott smiled at me warmly. Any "normal" friend of her daughter's was more than welcome. I supposed her parents had been knocked for six by SIB's revelations, too.

The rest of the day was wearying. I had to force myself not to gaze longingly at Nicola and could feel the same struggle in her. The shopping was obviously fruitless, but I did spring some of my precious money on a paisley dress for my "honeymoon" to make things look kosher. Luckily, Wendy ran out of steam, so we decided to call it a day and head home.

We caught the train back to Croydon, where the Scotts lived, and I had to turn on the charm all over again with Bob, Nicola's dad. A common love of football sorted that out, and we had a lively conversation over dinner about the First Division and how his team, Chelsea, was doing versus my own northern club of Newcastle United.

In between came queries about my Brian. Of course, I decided he was brave and handsome and in the Parachute Regiment, heading off for a tour of duty in Northern Ireland. I enjoyed watching Nicola's face as I invented my fiancé on the spot. I don't know how we held back our laughter. Nothing was mentioned about Nicola's military discharge, and I acted as if I had no idea of the past week's drama.

Wendy and Bob liked me and gradually unwound as we chatted and laughed around the dinner table. This was a family scarred by SIB's bald outing of their daughter and her subsequent dismissal from the armed forces. They were still in shock. Nicola was quiet and careful around them. She reeked of shame, hurt, and anger, and if I ever found out who had reported her, God help them. Careful, sensible Nicola, the one who'd always warned me, the one who'd tried to look out for me, could only have been betrayed by an informant. Her career as an army nurse was in tatters, a career she had excelled at and loved.

Once dinner was over, I insisted on washing up, and when I came back from the kitchen, Bob was pressing a twenty-quid note into Nicola's hand.

"Why don't you girls go and have a night out?" he said, his eyes on Nicola. "You need to blow the cobwebs away, don't you, love?" It was an act of kindness that brightened her for the first time since I'd arrived, and probably the first time since her world came crashing down.

Nicola showed me to her bedroom. There was one bed. "We have to share," she said tightly.

I gawped like a fool, waiting for a punchline. "Seriously?"

Nicola ignored me and rifled through her wardrobe for whatever she was going to wear that night. "This is my parents' house, Penny. After all I've been through, don't be so stupid."

Chastised, I opened my overnight case and unpacked. We dressed up for the bright lights, me in my new paisley purchase and Nicola in the blue dress I'd always loved on her and headed back up to London. Bob inadvertently sponsored my first visit to a London gay bar.

"I haven't seen my father look so happy since last Wednesday." Nicola told me on the train. "I know you came here to find out what's happened and how you're affected, but I have to thank you for today. You made them forget for a while. They like you. Even my mum was smiling."

I didn't know what to say, so I gave her hand a squeeze. The whole family was under massive strain. Nicola was their only child.

"I've disappointed them so much, Penny."

Tears trembled on her lashes and I pulled her into a hug.

"Stop that right now," I said. "Someone tipped Sibyl off. This is not your fault. You are a wonderful, gorgeous human being, and I love you, Nicola Scott," I whispered into her hair.

She pushed me gently away and a change came over her, a distancing of the physical, a refusal of what gave her comfort, what she really wanted. Needed. I could suddenly see the future ahead of her. One of conformity, of self-sacrifice, of walking on eggshells so as not to hurt her family. For the first time, my small, selfish heart truly broke.

"They found letters in my room," Nicola blurted, a new wave of shame crossing her face. "I wrote them to you after we broke up but out of silly pride, I suppose, never sent them." Her head dipped, her hands restless on her lap.

"What did they say?" My stomach went into knots. This was what I needed to know, but at the same time, didn't want to. It opened a wound between us that had never properly healed.

"Stupid stuff. That I loved you," she said. She stopped there, and I had the sense to wait. "Sexual stuff," she continued, after she'd composed herself. "Fantasies...whatever." Her face flamed. "But when they asked me about them, after they'd showed them to my parents, I denied you knew anything about it. I said we'd barely even spoken a word and that it was all in my mind. That I had these feelings for you, and the letters were my way to have a conversation I would never have the nerve to start."

"Oh, Nicola." I hurt for her on so any levels. That SIB had humiliated her in front of her parents, that she had lied to protect me, that our relationship had been in such a horrible state that she'd written those letters at all. I remembered Helen and Sandy and how SIB had instinctively known how to punish them on an emotional, as well as professional, level. It was a type of torture, as if they set out deliberately to destroy lives.

"You're safe, Penny. When they talk to you, just deny ever having met me outside of that one stay in the MRS. No one can say any different."

"Thank you for covering for me."

She gave me a weak smile. "I was the one got you into it in the first place."

We both knew that was a lie. I'd have found my way. I was a player, and today it felt like the loneliest game in the world.

We caught the tube to Sloane Square and walked up King's Road to the fire station. Nicola took my hand once we turned into a side and said, "Here it is."

Before me was a white wall with a green door. Unremarkable, though I wasn't sure what I was expecting.

"What is this place?" I asked.

"The Gateway Club," she said and rang the bell. Heavy footsteps echoed within. The door opened an inch or two and a short, very butch woman squinted at us suspiciously.

"Yeah. Are you members?"

"No. We're forces," Nicola answered.

"Come in, love." The door opened wide and we followed our host downstairs to a basement bar. "You gotta sign in." She pointed to a ledger.

I grabbed the pen and Nicola nudged me in the ribs. "Use a false name," she instructed.

I scribbled Judy Scragend and got a disapproving look from her.

"You'll never grow up."

I shrugged. "What's the hurry?" I went to get some drinks while Nicola snagged a corner table.

We sat, silently watching as more and more punters came in. I recognised a few from Guildford camp and was aware of the sideways glances we were getting, but no one came over.

"You'd think we were lepers." There was bitterness in my voice.

"They'll come around," Nicola assured me. "For the moment, we *are* lepers. SIB is all over us and we could easily cross-contaminate. That's what's worrying them."

I shook off my sulk and grabbed her hand. "Come on, let's dance. Let's show 'em how it's done."

As if on cue, Elton John's "Your Song" came on and we slid into the music cheek to cheek. It was divine. She was so soft in my arms and smelled so good. I found it hard to believe all the horrible things that had happened to us as we swayed together on the darkened dance floor, wrapped in our cocoon, watched by suspicious eyes.

On my next journey to the bar, Frances, a driver I knew from Guildford, came over to talk to me.

"How is she?" She nodded at Nicola.

"What do you think?" I had no time for snoopers. If she cared enough, she could ask Nicola herself.

"It's a bastard of a thing." The woman pulled out a

fiver and waved at the barwoman. "I'll get these." She bought our drinks. "Word is, she was dobbed in."

"I suspected as much." I relented slightly on remembering that Frances went out with an officer, so she had to be super careful. In the farthest, darkest corner, I thought I saw her squeeze along with a few other officer types though I didn't know any names. "I'd love to get my hands around her scrawny neck, whoever she is."

"Can't be too careful," Frances agreed. "Even a place like this—the only lesbian bar in London—can be dangerous if someone's got a grudge."

I collected my drinks to go and Frances said, "Give her my love, okay?"

"She's upset," I said, "but more for her parents. It was ugly the way SIB did it."

"Keep your own head down. Word is they're coming for you next."

I went back to my seat knowing every word she said was true. I was not out of the woods yet. Unlike Nicola, I had been lucky enough to be forewarned and could get my story straight. No matter what, I didn't want my time in the army to come to a sudden stop.

When I returned to our table, Nicola asked what Frances had wanted. I told her the whole conversation, leaning in close to be heard over the music, and suddenly we were kissing. Despite her sadness, Nicola's kisses were deep and sexy and very intense. My body immediately responded, and I wanted to get her somewhere quiet and rip her clothes off. Like in the old days, when I couldn't get enough of her, when my eagerness had been too transparent, too immediate...too stupid. Who had snitched on us? I couldn't understand why someone would do that. Hadn't I been told over and over to be careful? And had I listened? I could have howled my guilt to the moon for all the good it would do now.

The evening provided the distraction we both needed. We danced and drank, and I wanted her so much. I ached for it to be the way it was before all the pain arrived.

At one in the morning, we sneaked into Nicola's house as quiet as mice. Nicola held my hand as she led me upstairs. She was tipsy, and I could imagine the old Nicola—my Nicola—shimmering under the surface of her soft, pale skin. In her room, we stood facing each other, looking into each other's eyes. She finally saw me. The truth of the feelings I had for her, and also the immature ego-fuelled foolishness that would forever sabotage my life. I was a flawed being, and in her eyes shining back at me, I knew she saw it all yet loved me anyway. She kissed me.

Aware that her parents were sleeping in a nearby room, we made love quietly and gently all through what was left of the night.

When the new day broke, I cradled her in my arms and cried.

The End

About the Author

Penny Taylor lives in Robin Hood country, also known as Nottingham, UK. Though, as a compulsive traveller, she is seldom there. When not globetrotting, she can be found watching or playing all kinds of sports and is killer at backgammon.

Coming Soon from Dirt Road Books

Big Girl Pill
by KD Williamson

Maya Davis is done hiding. It's left her empty and out of touch with her family. Now she's a young woman on a mission: getting rid of residual feelings for her former best friend from college. Her plan is to put herself through a wringer by being in Nina's upcoming wedding and burning away whatever emotions are left, so she can start anew. Her plan, however, has big holes, and everything she's been feeling rushes through and leaves her thinking that this was a bad idea.

Nina Sterling is a work in progress, torn between being two very different things—the person others expect her to be and who she wants to become. For the past couple of years, it's been easier to give in to her demanding, steamroller of a mother and her pleasant but controlling fiancé, but with Maya's return for a lengthy stay in town, and encouragement from Nina's hilarious cousin, seeds of rebellion are sown.

As Maya and Nina try to patch up the past and get closer, old sparks rekindle, and as they both grow into who they are meant to be, those sparks might just become a fire.

South Paw
Garoul Book 6
by Gill McKnight

As an introvert and a germaphobe, Elizabeth Wren is struggling in her new job, working for Martha Meeke, the flamboyant literary agent. Now their most famous client, bestselling Priscila Purloin, has gone AWOL, and Elizabeth is dispatched to South Paw, a skiing resort famous for its beautiful Christmas ambience, to track her down. Luckily, Elizabeth also suffers from OCD—obsessive Christmas disorder—so maybe South Paw will not be a washout after all. Naeva Garoul dreads snow season, when her tranquil mountain home becomes a Mecca for ski sport enthusiasts and Christmas-themed lunacy. Winter means family visits, too, and when your family consists of werewolves, it usually involves chaos. Werewolves want to hunt deer, run in the woods, and howl at the moon, while all Naeva wants to do is sit by the fire, write, and eat broccoli. It's hard being a vegetarian werewolf, never mind a romance novelist who wants to be alone.

Rise and Shine
by Jove Belle

For best friends Emily and Sarah, a zombie outbreak seems like a pretty good reason to skip third period. And to skip town, for that matter. The girls pack up and start out on a 400-mile road trip to a bunker Emily's survivalist dad built. With a little luck, they'll survive long enough to make it to safety, and maybe fall in love along the way.

Welcome to the Wallops
(Second Ed.)
by Gill McKnight

The villages of High Wallop and Lesser Wallop have graced either end of the Wallop valley since medieval times. And competition between the two has never ceased since, especially over the famous Cheese and Beer Festival.

As festival manager, Jane Swallow has always struggled to maintain peace and equanimity within the community she loves, but this year everything is wrong. Her irascible father has just been released from jail, her job is on the line, and to top it all, her ex-girlfriend has just moved in next door.

Her life is going to hell in a handcart, unless she can pull off some sort of miracle.

Queen of the Glens
by Gill McKnight

Alecka Kruche's brother, Howie, has gone AWOL in Ireland. AWOL is not an unusual state for Howie, and his level-headed sister is dispatched to collar him and return him home. Again.

But this time, it's different. Howie has fallen in love. As Alecka tries to extract him from the village of Inish Og in the beautiful Glens of Antrim on the north Irish coast, she instead finds herself drawn in. The folklore, culture, and sheer magic of the Glens begin to break down her reserve. She's charmed—and entirely unsure what to do about it—by the villagers and by Johneen, a headstrong woman who isn't nearly as charmed by Alecka.

Borage
Book 1 in Sisters of the 13th Moon Series
by Gill McKnight

Astral is the last of the Projector witches on a special mission to find an evil critter that is damaging her coven. Her search brings her to Black & Blacker, a company run by the enigmatic Abby Black. But who is bewitching who?

A Matter of Blood

Far Seek Chronicles 2 (Second Ed.)

by Andi Marquette

Outlaw Torri Rendego can't shake her past, which most often involves Kai Tinsdale, her former Academy bunkmate and now commander in the hated Coalition forces. Torri's convinced that the Coalition is up to no good on Kai's family holdings and decides to investigate. Problem is, the Coalition is definitely up to something, and Torri and the crew of the Far Seek have to pursue an outrageous plan to gather information and pass it along to Kai somehow.

But even the best-laid plans can go dangerously awry, especially where Kai's concerned. Risking herself, her crew, and a tenuous tie to a shared history, Torri goes deep into Coalition territory to uncover a secret with far-reaching consequences for a distant and ancient culture. The stakes of this venture may prove way too high, even for a gambler like Torri.

Hollister Investigations:
The Shell Game

by Jove Belle

Since coming to work for Laila at Hollister Investigations, Trinity finds herself in a rut. She misses the excitement of being a hacktivist, and the tedium of investigating unfaithful spouses does nothing to stimulate her brain. But the inexplicable and undeniable pull of Laila Hollister keeps Trinity in her orbit, and she can't leave until she figures out what that means.

Laila is happy. Or as close to happy as she can get. Her company is solid and growing, her employees are elite at what they do, and adding Trinity to the roster only increased their earnings. But she makes Laila crazy, in ways that Laila can't understand. When rumors that Trinity might regret working there reach Laila, she lets Trinity work a case pro bono, just to make Trinity happy. Together they uncover layers of corrupt employees, identity theft, and bank fraud, and work to protect the vulnerable patients at the care facility where Trinity's Alzheimer's-affected mom lives.

Sweet and Sour

Book 1 in The Culinary School Series
by R.G. Emanuelle

Giovanna (Jo) Rossini is graduating from culinary school, but just as she's about to realize her dream of opening up a restaurant, her six-year relationship with Brenda starts to fall apart. Afraid that Brenda is resentful of the financial burden that's been placed on her, Jo begins to suspect that she's having an affair.

Sofia Gibb is dubious when the owner of the lesbian bar she manages wants to turn it into an eatery. Reluctantly, she goes to several restaurants to review sample menus, including the one where Jo is interning. There's an instant spark, but Jo is in a relationship and too preoccupied with her plans to deal with her feelings.

In the whirlwind of a restaurant opening, a fracturing relationship, and an attraction that she can't do anything about, Jo tries to keep her business afloat and herself together. In this prequel to the novella Add Spice to Taste, we visit with Jo again and join her on the journey that leads her to The New York Culinary Institute.

Also from Dirt Road Books

Fianna the Gold
Book 1 of the Shift Series
by Louisa Kelley

Abbie's life hasn't made much sense. She doesn't understand why she's a compulsive thief or why weird things keep happening to her. One night, mysterious men show up at her campsite seeking to capture her. She escapes, but there's a blank in her memory and she has no idea how she got away or what the men may have wanted.

Fianna, a dragon with the House of Gold, and her two sisters, Orla and Guin, are on a mission to locate a human-dragon hybrid and deliver her to the dragon community. That hybrid is Abbie. However, their plans are complicated when they discover that Abbie is also being hunted by a human who wants to harness Abbie's special powers for financial gain, as well as by a centuries-old dragon who wants to control the hybrid.

If Abbie wants to find out who she really is, she'll need to make a choice about who to trust and what secrets to hold.

Learning Curve:
Stories of Lessons Learned

An Anthology
Various Authors

Building a house, rebuilding a relationship, finding your purpose, learning archery, relearning the piano, discovering your family lineage, going on a journey, learning to face tragedy, teaching a kid to play ball, uncovering a truth in your heart, paying your dues on a ski slope. These are all themes that can be found in Learning Curve, and they are all lessons of one kind or another. The characters in these stories learn skills, life lessons, and how to open up to love and friendship.

This anthology of short stories brings together some of your favorite authors, as well as new writers who we're sure you'll enjoy. Our contributors include: Lori Lake, Sacchi Green, KD Williamson, Jessie Chandler, Stefani Deoul, Catherine Lane, Anna Burke, Michelle Teichman, Jove Belle, Andi Marquette, and R.G. Emanuelle.

Dirt Road Books is proud to donate all proceeds from this anthology to One Girl, an organization dedicated to educating and advancing the lives of girls around the world.

Wild Rides

by Sacchi Green

Sex, adventure, and wild rides—some literal, some journeys of the mind and heart. There's something for everyone here. How about a mechanical bull at a country-and-western bar in the Amsterdam of the 1980s? An army jeep in Vietnam in the '60s? A Chinese pirate ship far out in the Pacific in the '30s? A hot air balloon soaring above post-Civil War Wyoming? These rides transport you through time, as well as space. In more contemporary settings, you can find (and feel) pent-up passion behind prison walls, a reunion of rivals in a steaming sauna, and a couple both wounded and bonded by modern warfare. There's plenty of lust and banter, as well as mighty draft horses, at a county fair, and a visit with honeymooners in Paris with a fetish for gargoyles. Add to this mix a ghost story on a Montana ranch, a lovely vampire in the Old West, the occasional dragon, and a noir tale of sex, life, and afterlife in New York City. In Sacchi Green's second collection of her own work, you have all the variety, intriguing characters, and seamless merging of sex and story that she's required in the many anthologies she's edited.

The Potion
by R.G. Emanuelle

A secret formula. A mysterious blue potion. A woman determined to perfect an experiment that will change everything for women in an era when women are not free to choose. In the tradition of mad scientists, Vera Kennedy will stop at nothing to create the elixir that will give women the power to live according to their own desires. But when Georgette Harris comes to her with a plea for help in finding the key that could rescue her from destitution, Vera is pleasantly distracted. Together, they will unravel a mystery that includes ghostly elements and unscrupulous men.

Little Dip
Garoul Book 5
by Gill McKnight

It's 1977, and Connie Fortune has an easy, freewheeling life as a wildlife illustrator. A contract with a periodical brings her to Little Dip, but a clash with Marie Garoul ruins the deal. Next year, Connie tries again—but Marie is waiting for her.

Friends in High Places
Far Seek Chronicles 1 (Second Ed.)
by Andi Marquette

Outlaw Torri Rendego and her crew are working to fulfill a black market contract on Old Earth, but they have to contend with hated Coalition forces. Kai Tinsdale, a part of Torri's past she never expected to see again, shows up, and Torri's survival depends on their ability to trust one another.

Bitterroot Queen
by Jove Belle

Sam Marconi and her teenage daughter move to Bitterroot, Idaho, to open a motel, but they find it in a derelict state. Sam posts an ad in town for someone to help her with renovations. Olly Jones, another newcomer to the area, is the only one who shows up for the job, even though her first meeting with Sam went badly. Sam hires her regardless, and eventually realizes that Olly is exactly what she needs to save the Bitterroot Queen. Will they find a way to build the life they've both been searching for? Or will they cling to the ties holding them to the past?

Lightning Source UK Ltd.
Milton Keynes UK
UKHW020643141119
353525UK00010B/699/P